DATE DUE

Abortion on Trial

——————————————————— RUSSELL SHAW

Abortion on Trial

PFLAUM PRESS
DAYTON, OHIO
1968

Nihil Obstat: Rev. John C. Selner, S.S., S.T.D.
Censor Librorum
Imprimatur: ✛ Patrick Cardinal O'Boyle
Archbishop of Washington
February 16, 1968

The *nihil obstat* and *imprimatur* are official declarations
that a book or pamphlet is free of doctrinal or moral error.
No implication is contained therein that those who have
granted the *nihil obstat* and the *imprimatur* agree with the
contents, opinions or statements expressed.

For my wife and children

ACKNOWLEDGMENTS

The author wishes to acknowledge permission to use the following copyrighted material:

Richard A. McCormick, S.J., "Abortion." Reprinted with permission from AMERICA, The National Catholic Weekly Review, June 19, 1965. All rights reserved. Copyright © America Press, Inc., 106 West 56 Street, New York, New York, 1965.

From *Catholic Viewpoint on Overpopulation*, by Anthony Zimmerman. Copyright 1961 by Anthony Zimmerman. Reprinted by permission of Doubleday & Company, Inc.

From *Moral Dilemmas*, by Gerald Vann. Copyright © 1965 by Mark Brocklehurst. Reprinted by permission of Doubleday & Company, Inc.

From the book *Medicine and Morals*, by John Marshall, M. D. Copyright © 1960 by Hawthorn Books, Inc. Published by Hawthorn Books, Inc., 70 Fifth Avenue, New York, New York.

From *Abortion*, copyright © 1966 by Lawrence Lader, reprinted by permission of the publishers, The Bobbs-Merrill Company, Inc.

David T. Smith, editor, *Abortion and the Law* (Cleveland: The Press of Case Western Reserve University, 1967).

Paul H. Gebhard, Wardell B. Pomeroy, Clyde E. Martin, Cornelia V. Christenson, *Pregnancy, Birth and Abortion* (New York: Harper Brothers, 1958).

Mary Steichen Calderone, M. D., editor, *Abortion in the United States* (New York: Harper Brothers, 1958).

David Lowe, *Abortion and the Law* (New York: Pocket Books, 1966).

Abortion, An Ethical Discussion, copyright Central Board of Finance of the Church of England (London, 1965).

From *New Catholic Encyclopedia*, Volumes 5 and 13. Copyright © 1967 by The Catholic University of America, Washington, D.C. Used by permission of McGraw-Hill Book Co.

Eugene Quay, "Justifiable Abortion," *The Georgetown Law Journal*, Vol. 49, No. 62 (Winter, 1960) and No. 3 (Spring, 1961).

Anthony Zimmerman, S.V.D., "An Abortion Explosion in Japan", *U.S. Catholic*, May, 1965.

Paul Ramsey, "The Sanctity of Life: In the First of It," *The Dublin Review*, Spring, 1967. With permission of *The Tablet*, London.

Robert M. Byrn, "Abortion in Perspective," *Duquesne University Law Review*, Vol. 5, No. 2 (Winter 1966-67).

Garrett Hardin, "The History and Future of Birth Control," *Perspectives in Biology and Medicine*. Vol. 10, No. 1 (Autumn 1966). Used by permission of the publisher, The University of Chicago Press.

Paul Ferris, *The Nameless: Abortion in Britain Today*, 1966. Used with the permission of the Hutchinson Publishing Group Ltd., London, and Curtis Brown Ltd., London.

Commonweal Publishing Co. Inc. of New York for various articles quoted.

Ruth Link, "Those New Swedish Abortion Pills," *Ladies' Home Journal*, June, 1967.

Bernard Berelson, editor, *Family Planning and Population Programs: A Review of World Developments*. Chicago, University of Chicago Press, 1966. Copyright © 1966 by the University of Chicago.

Group for the Advancement of Psychiatry, *Sex and the College Student*, New York, 1965.

Arthur McCormack, editor, *Christian Responsibility and World Poverty*, 1963. Used with permission of Paulist/Newman Press, New York.

Cahal B. Daly, *Natural Law Morality Today*, Dublin, Clonmore & Reynolds, Ltd., and London, Burns & Oates, Ltd., 1965.

Thomas S. Szasz, M.D., "The Ethics of Abortion," from *The Humanist*. Copyright © by the American Humanist Association, 125 El Camino del Mar, San Francisco, California. Reprinted by permission.

Contents

I

INTRODUCTION:
Time for A Change?

"Babies," remarked Mrs. Jill Knight, a Conservative Member of Parliament from the Edgbaston section of Birmingham, during a debate in the House of Commons in 1966, "are not like bad teeth to be jerked out just because they cause suffering. An unborn baby is a baby nevertheless."[1]

"There ought to be no special laws regulating abortion," wrote psychiatrist Dr. Thomas S. Szasz in 1966. "Such an operation should be available in the same way as, say, an operation for the beautification of a nose: the only requirement ought to be the woman's desire to have the operation, her consent, and the willingness of a physician to perform the procedure."[2]

These two statements mark out clearly the issues at stake in the debate on abortion, a debate which in the past few years has spread throughout the United States and engaged the attention of legislators, doc-

[1] Parliamentary Debates (Hansard), House of Commons, Vol. 732, No. 60 (July 22, 1966), 1100.
[2] Thomas S. Szasz, M.D., "The Ethics of Abortion," *Humanist*, September/October, 1966.

1

tors, clergymen and concerned laymen. Central to
this debate are two radically opposed views of the
unborn child and his rights. On the one hand there
is the view which sees the child before birth as a
being in full possession of inalienable and inviolable
rights, above all the right to life. On the other there
is the view which sees the unborn child as something
less than human, perhaps no more than—in Dr.
Szasz's terminology—"a part of the mother's body,"
and which therefore possesses no rights which cannot, at least under certain circumstances, be violated
for the safety, well-being or possibly only the convenience of its parents, or society at large.

This debate has not been taking place in the
abstract. It has instead centered on a practical political question: should existing laws on abortion, which
in most states are fairly stringent, be relaxed to make
abortions easier to obtain. This legislative controversy has been conducted with deadly earnestness;
yet any argument about abortion laws is essentially
illogical. Dr. Szasz has stated the matter quite clearly: "If abortion is murder—as Roman Catholics and
some others quite reasonably maintain—it is an
immoral act which the law must prohibit." On the
other hand, if abortion is not murder, if in fact it
has no more significance than the sort of cosmetic
surgery mentioned by Dr. Szasz, then there is no
reason why it should be the concern of the law at
all. In that case, "the proper remedy must be sought
not in medically and psychiatrically 'liberal' abortion

laws, but in the repeal of all such laws."[3] The law, one might say, should not tolerate even a small amount of murder; but neither should it take any notice of the removal of a bit of excess, non-human tissue from a woman's womb.

It is the contention of this book that what is removed from the womb in an abortion is not a small quantity of non-human tissue, but a being possessed of all the rights of a human person, in particular the right to life. If this is true, then abortion—*all* abortion—may properly be called homicide. And those who accept this point of view need not logically go further in justifying—to themselves, at any rate—their opposition to efforts to make it easier to obtain abortions. Obviously, however, many people do not accept this view of the fetus. One purpose of this book will be to demonstrate that it is not only, in Dr. Szasz's phrase, a "quite reasonable" view, but that it is in fact the only consistent and morally tenable view.

The argument against abortion does not, however, rest solely on moral grounds, a fortunate thing in an era when consensus on many moral issues is hard to come by. Abortion is also a highly dubious practice medically and psychiatrically, while from the point of view of society it is fraught with dangerous consequences. It will therefore be a further purpose of this book to examine the medical, psychiatric and social aspects of the question in order to demonstrate that abortion can and should be opposed for many reasons besides those of sound morality.

[3]*Ibid.*

Fundamentally, however, one comes back to that central question: what do you make of the unborn child? Is the fetus an inanimate lump of tissue? Or is it a person? The law can have nothing to say about what parents and doctors choose to do with inanimate tissue. But the law cannot afford to tolerate any violation of a human person's right to life.

THE PRESSURE FOR CHANGE

Two years ago, in preparing a shorter study of the abortion problem,[4] the present writer found it necessary to document the mounting pressure for relaxation of American laws against abortion by listing a number of articles which had appeared in popular magazines. But many things can change in two years, and documentation of the pressure for relaxing the abortion laws would now be entirely superfluous as well as being hopelessly out of date before it could ever get into print. The mass media is saturated with treatments of the issue, most of it more or less favorable to lowering or leveling the present barriers against abortion. The subject is discussed on television and radio. Articles by the score appear in mass circulation magazines and newspapers, as well as in medical, psychiatric and sociological journals. No one today could possibly be ignorant of the fact that an extremely well-publicized campaign is being waged for liberalization of the laws against abortion.

[4]Russell B. Shaw, *Abortion and Public Policy* (Washington, 1966).

Agitation for the relaxation of existing state laws has been a fact of American life for the past decade or more. In the past three or four years, however, the agitation has increased, and in 1967 it began to score notable successes. In 1967 Colorado became the first state in the country to enact legislation along the lines advocated by the "reformers." It was followed soon after by North Carolina and California. During 1967 bills for legislative changes or for study commissions on the question were introduced in twenty other states. Citizens of those states where the debate has not yet reached the state legislature can be certain that it will do so in the immediate future.

A number of national, state and local groups advocating relaxation of the abortion laws have sprung up. The Association for the Study of Abortion with headquarters in New York City was founded in 1964. Its president is Dr. Robert Hall, Associate Professor of Obstetrics at Columbia-Presbyterian Medical Center. Other prestigious names associated with the ASA include Cass Canfield, former chairman of the executive committee of Harper & Row; the Rev. Joseph F. Fletcher, Professor of Christian Ethics at the Episcopal Theological School, Cambridge, Massachusetts; and Dr. Alan F. Guttmacher, president of the Planned Parenthood Federation. On the West Coast there is the Society for Humane Abortion with headquarters in San Francisco, which sponsored, among other activities, a conference on abortion and human rights in January, 1966. The foundress of the SHA is

Patricia Maginnis, a confirmed abortion crusader who in July, 1966, dramatized her cause by being arrested outside the State Building in San Francisco for distributing leaflets and enrolling women in abortion classes.[5]

Smaller groups have also entered the field of abortion reform. Easily the most colorful, at least in its prose style, is an organization called Legalize Abortion, which operates from a post office box number in Los Angeles. Though the literature distributed by Legalize Abortion manifests many of the characteristics of what could only be called—politely —a fringe group, it does offer some interesting insights into the mentality of the hard-core pro-abortion crusaders.

A twenty-six page, single-spaced set of mimeographed instructions from Legalize Abortion entitled "How To Set Up a Legalize Abortion Committee" covers everything from running a fund-raising social, through pressure and propaganda campaigns aimed at communications media and legislators, to detailed information on how to conduct public demonstrations.[6]

A special section tells how to establish campus committees. "The function of campus groups," it says, "is to see to it that all persons presently in high schools, junior high schools, and in grammar schools

[5]*The San Francisco Chronicle*, July 26, 1966.
[6]*How To Set Up a Legalize Abortion Committee*, second edition (mimeographed). Distributed by Legalize Abortion, Los Angeles, California.

are in favor of legalization of abortion."

Legalize Abortion makes no bones about its aim: "without resorting to civil disobedience, to make abortion legally available on demand." This, it stresses, will only be accomplished by broad political action. "This pamphlet," the instructions read, "contains no advice that is properly labeled nonpolitical (except for instance suggestions that your group hold socials occasionally). We regard claiming to be nonpolitical and opposing antiabortion penal codes as pure fraud."

The first page of the instructions carries a statement—capitalized—as a "point to remember": "NEITHER YOU NOR ANYONE ELSE HAS ANY OBLIGATION TO APOLOGIZE EITHER FOR HIS BELIEFS OR FOR HIS PREFERENCES— WHATEVER THESE MAY BE."

The document does not say specifically that campaigning for abortion will mean fighting Catholics, but it seems to assume this and gives advice accordingly. Counseling local activists to "make enough noise to let the public know you exist," it says: "If necessary, you picket Roman Catholic Churches." It also offers this suggestion for getting attention: "If you have 'phone in and talk' shows on your local radio stations, you can call in and raise the issue of legalization of abortion or more conservatively of the high rate of illegal abortion in the U.S. This will result in Roman Catholics calling in and calling abortion murder. One way of handling the latter is to have someone else call in and raise the issue early in the show, then let two or three Roman Catholics go through the murder routine, and then call up and refute them."

The instructions call for the creation of "self-sufficient pressure groups" working to legalize abortion. An "established pressure group" is defined as "one capable of putting up a picket line or passing out literature anywhere within a 50-mile radius given four hours' notice and capable of mimeographing 10,000 pages of literature given 24 hours' notice." The ultimate objective of such groups, the document states, is to win passage of "remedial legislation legalizing abortion—by whatever combination of nonviolent political tactics that prove to be most expedient."

The document offers this advice on the appearance of demonstrators: "No sandals or bare feet. Skirts on women. Males: white shirt and tie or shirt without coat. Males: hair very short by ears. Women: long hair done up (not hanging over shoulders)." It suggests a number of stock answers for demonstrators accosted by indignant citizens. Sample: "The quickest way to reduce the number of abortions is to legalize abortion. Only then will the Roman Catholic Church remove its opposition to teaching contraception in the grammar schools."

Far out as some of this may sound, no one should be tempted to dismiss it casually. Legalize Abortion and its Los Angeles post office box may or may not be significant factors in the current pro-abortion campaign. What matters is that the idea of abortion is currently being advocated in this country with remarkable success. A *Wall Street Journal* reviewer of the book *Abortion* by Lawrence Lader, another veteran abortion crusader and a member of the Board of Directors of the Association for the Study of Abortion, stated the problem well:

> While some may dismiss such books and remarks as poppycock, it may be better to recall that, not so many years ago those calling for freedom to use birth control devices were regarded as cranks, with little chance of having their views accepted by the nation. In the last few years, of course, this group has won decisively—even to the point where the Federal Government is moving to sponsor birth control services.
> Many of those who fought for free use of contraceptives have now turned to the fight for free abortion, and they're using the same techniques—speeches, magazine articles, books, resolutions presented to all kinds of associations, court cases and amendments to laws—to raise the abortion issue. If for no other reason than this effort, the American public is going to have to make up its mind on the issues involved.[7]

One segment of the American public which has made up its mind is the influential American Medical Association, or at least its policy-making House of Delegates. On June 21, 1967, the 242-member House, in the face of what was described as "significant but inadequate" opposition, went on record in favor of

[7]William M. Carley in *The Wall Street Journal*, June 6, 1966.

liberalized abortion laws.[8] The action reversed a ninety-six-year policy of the Association. A report by a committee favoring the new stand noted that doctors performed 10,000 abortions annually in accredited hospitals, but that few of these were necessary to save the life of the mother, the sole circumstance in which abortion was legally permitted in most places. In performing the bulk of these abortions, the report stated, physicians were acting "contrary to existing laws," and this put such doctors in an "uncomfortable" position.

WHY CHANGE IS SOUGHT

One recent writer on the subject of abortion listed three principal considerations behind the position of those who advocate a broadening of the abortion laws.[9] First, premarital sexual relations are more common today than perhaps ever before. The result is an increase in the number of illegitimate pregnancies, and easier abortion is sought as a way of avoiding the disgrace or inconvenience of illegitimacy. Second, pregnancies sometimes occur even among those who habitually use contraceptives. "No matter how effective the contraceptive," one study put it, "unwanted pregnancies will occur, and when all else fails, abortion may be the only answer."[10]

[8]*The New York Times,* June 22, 1966.
[9]Richard A. McCormick, S.J., "Abortion," *America,* June 19, 1965.
[10]Kenneth R. Niswander and Morton Klein, quoted in Lawrence Lader, *Abortion* (New York, 1966), p. 151.

In such cases, the already established determination of one or both parents to prevent the birth of a child tends to predispose them to abortion when contraception fails. Finally, the pressure of easing restrictions on abortions is said to be aimed at depriving illegal abortionists of their business, which comes to them, it is asserted, because stringent abortion laws leave many people with no other recourse.

All these reasons are operative in the attitudes of those who advocate easier abortion. But a fourth consideration motivating some of those most active in the campaign deserves attention. It is the argument that the choice of abortion is a woman's right, with which no one else should be allowed to interfere.

Several variations are played upon this theme, sometimes by the same source. In some contexts, freedom of abortion is viewed as a civil right: "the one just and inevitable answer to the quest for feminine freedom."[11] Elsewhere a religious note is sounded; freedom of abortion is said to embody "the supreme morality of our time, the guarantee that every child shall become a wanted child."[12] (One observer, commenting on the "wanted child" argument, remarked: "That is very nice if one can arrange it, but to do so one has to choose one's parents extremely carefully."[13])

[11]Lader, 169.
[12]Lader, 170.
[13]Norman St. John-Stevas in Parliamentary Debates (Hansard), House of Commons, Vol. 732, No. 60 (July 22, 1966), 1154.

The rights of physicians are also cited as justifying freedom of abortion. Dr. Hall, president of the Association for the Study of Abortion, has argued that doctors should be spared the hard burden of deciding whether or not a particular abortion is needed or justified, since "we are no more qualified to do so than accountants or street cleaners."[14] Removal of all legal restrictions on abortions will also soothe the consciences of the parents, according to Dr. Hall; they will be "spared a great deal of otherwise inevitable guilt if their society sanctions what they do."[15]

In short, for some of those most firmly committed to the fight for relaxation of abortion laws, the only real solution, as we saw Dr. Szasz argue, is to remove all laws. This will exempt doctors from having to make painful decisions and will assure parents who choose abortion that their choice is socially acceptable. Above all, it will mark the final stage in feminine emancipation: "The ultimate freedom remains the right of every woman to legalized abortion."[16]

It is worth noting in this connection that, despite the frequent mention in pro-abortion propaganda of pregnant, mentally defective, thirteen-year-old girls who have been raped by their fathers, the vast majority of women who undergo abortions are married, pregnant by their husbands, middle-class and

[14]Robert E. Hall, M.D., quoted in Lader, 168.
[15]Hall, quoted in Lader, 169.
[16]Lader, 167.

mothers of other children. Dr. Harold Rosen, a prominent advocate of legalized abortion, writes:

> In the United States nine-tenths or more of all artificially induced abortions, whether therapeutic or criminal, are procured or prescribed for married women, impregnated by their husbands, with three or more children, and over thirty years of age. If legal, they are performed ostensibly for medical or psychiatric reasons; if illegal, the reasons alleged may, perhaps, also be medical or psychiatric. Whether legal or illegal, nevertheless, the reasons, but not the rationalizations advanced, may be, and usually are, socioeconomic.[17]

Despite its quasi-scientific pretensions, the word "socioeconomic" is, to say the least, ambiguous. "Socioeconomic" grounds for abortion can refer to the situation of the forty-year-old mother of five children whose husband earns $6,500 a year and who has just learned that she is pregnant again. But the same term can be applied to the situation of the newly pregnant thirty-year-old mother of two whose husband earns $15,000 a year and who has been counting on a trip to Europe next summer if the budget and family circumstances will permit. Some of those who have considered the question seem to think the latter is the more common case. A report by a Church of England body points to studies which show that the highest incidence of induced abortion occurs among "the urban, better-educated, higher-

---

[17]Harold Rosen, M.D., "Psychiatric Implications of Abortion: A Case Study in Social Hypocrisy," in David T. Smith, ed., *Abortion and the Law* (Cleveland, 1967), p. 78.

income groups."[18] In such circumstances necessity has little or nothing to do with the case; abortion is performed only for the sake of convenience.

Two recent, internationally publicized events have focused attention on the abortion issue to an unprecedented degree and quickened the pace of activity for relaxation of the laws. Neither, it should be said, has anything to do with the sort of "convenience" abortions described above. In each, genuine human tragedies occurred. These have been appealed to as justification for making it easier to obtain abortions. The first was the birth in Europe of some 5,000 to 7,000 deformed children whose mothers had taken the tranquilizing drug thalidomide during pregnancy. The other was an epidemic of rubella (German measles) which swept the United States in 1964 and 1965, leaving in its wake an estimated 20,000 infants with various defects caused by their mothers' contracting the disease early in pregnancy.

THE THALIDOMIDE TRAGEDY

Probably the most widely noted incident connected with the thalidomide disaster was the November, 1962, trial in Liège, Belgium, of Mrs. Suzanne van de Put, accused of murdering her infant daughter, Corinne. Mrs. van de Put had taken eleven

[18]*Abortion, An Ethical Discussion,* published for the Church Assembly Board for Social Responsibility by the Church Information Office (London, 1965), p. 10.

thalidomide pills prescribed to her before she became pregnant. On May 22, 1962, her daughter was born with no arms or shoulder structure and with deformed feet. Soon after, the mother administered to the child a fatal barbiturate mixed with honey and water. She did not deny having killed Corinne but argued that she had acted in order to save her child from a lifetime of suffering. After six dramatic days in the courtroom, reported in newspapers throughout the world, Mrs. van de Put was acquitted by twelve male jurors. There was a public celebration inside and outside the courtroom, and traffic in central Liège was tied up for more than an hour.

The death of Corinne van de Put did not involve abortion. It did, however, raise closely analogous issues. The central question in the case is also at the heart of the debate over abortion: whether anyone, for however apparently reasonable or humane a cause, has the right directly to destroy innocent human life.

Closer to home, the thalidomide tragedy was dramatized in the case of Mrs. Sherri Finkbine of Phoenix, Arizona. During pregnancy Mrs. Finkbine had taken thalidomide purchased by her husband in London. (With the exception of a few test samples, the drug was kept out of the United States through the vigilance of Dr. Frances Kelsey of the United States Food and Drug Administration.) In July, 1962, a physicians' panel recommended that she be permitted to undergo an abortion rather than risk giving birth to a deformed child. Subsequently, however, the county medical society refused to sanction the abortion until legal aspects of the case had been settled. Arizona law, like that of most states, forbade abortion except to save the life of the mother. The local superior court then rejected a suit filed by Mrs. Finkbine seeking permission for the abortion. Feeling "caught in a frenzy of frustration, impatience, and mounting terror,"[19] she sought a visa to go to Japan, where abortions on demand are available to both Japanese and foreigners. When it appeared that there would be a delay in obtaining the visa, she and her husband flew to Stockholm, where abortions had been performed on women who had taken thalidomide. The operation took place soon after. Mrs. Finkbine was advised by the doctor that the child would have been badly deformed had it lived.

THE RUBELLA EPIDEMIC

The problem of deformed children, and abortion as a proposed solution, are also intimately involved in the agitation accompanying the rubella epidemic in the United States during 1964 and 1965. Estimates vary widely on the percentage of children who will suffer from defects as a result of their mothers' having contracted the disease during pregnancy. Some early figures, based on retrospective studies that concentrated on damaged children, put this at a staggering ninety percent or more. By contrast, others state

[19]Lader, 15.

that severe congenital defects are present in only one out of every five or six such cases. One careful study of 227 children born to mothers who contracted rubella in pregnancy found an incidence of mental retardation no higher than for the general population.[20]

A recent authoritative study based in part on the American epidemic concluded that women who contract rubella in the first month of pregnancy run up to a forty percent risk of having children with defects; if, however, the disease comes in the third month, the risk may fall as low as ten percent.[21] It is established that rubella early in pregnancy may result in the birth of children with such defects as cataracts, deaf-mutism, cardiac anomalies and mental retardation. But it is also established that a child born to a mother who has had the disease during pregnancy may suffer no defects or only minor and correctable ones.[22]

Nevertheless the possibility of severe defects in the child has led to a campaign of agitation for abortion in cases where fetal damage as a result of rubella is judged likely, a campaign marred by the "superficiality and over-simplication" deplored by one prominent medical educator as characteristic of the

[20]Kenneth J. Ryan, M.D., "Humane Abortion Laws and the Health Needs of Society," in Smith, 65.

[21]*The Washington Post,* August 30, 1965; *Time,* September 17, 1965.

[22]Ryan in Smith, 65.

debate on abortion.[23] *Life* magazine speedily decreed an "almost 50-50 chance" of deformities in such cases and presented the plight of women who seek abortion in these circumstances in highly sympathetic terms.[24] The magazine also gave a pat on the back to physicians who performed abortions on these grounds, calling them "conscientious doctors of highest integrity who acted in defiance of community convention and state law."

Other "conscientious doctors of highest integrity" have, however, questioned the reasonableness of abortion in cases of German measles. Dr. Isadore Dyer, Chief of Obstetrics at Charity Hospital in New Orleans, commented: "If between ten percent and twenty percent of the women who contract the disease in these first three months are going to have babies with anomalies, it seems rather drastic to destroy the other eighty percent or ninety percent to guard against this."[25] Put another way, one might ask how great a statistical risk of having a defective child is to be presumed to be justification for killing an unborn child. *Life*'s "50-50 chance"? A three-to-one likelihood? Four-to-one? Or is it possible that where human life is at stake the question should

[23]Andre E. Hellegers, M.D., "Law and the Common Good," *Commonweal*, June 30, 1967.

[24]*Life*, June 4, 1965. *Life*'s account centered on a Catholic woman whose abortion allegedly was condoned by several priests. When the priests involved filed a libel suit, the magazine printed a "correction" stating it had been "misinformed" on this point.

[25]*Time*, September 17, 1965.

not be settled on the basis of a decision by odds-makers? One of the curious things about the pressure for easier abortion on grounds of rubella-caused defects is that researchers are presently developing a vaccine to confer immunity against the disease before its next epidemic outbreak.[26] It seems farfetched to advocate a drastic measure like liberalizing the abortion laws on the grounds that it is needed to cope with the consequences of a disease which science expects to have virtually eradicated before its next major outbreak.

It should, of course, be noted that abortion in cases of rubella or other situations where fetal defects are suspected—for example, when a woman has been exposed to X-rays in the area of the womb early in pregnancy—are, protestations to the contrary notwithstanding, not a service to the child but are meant rather to serve the convenience or the aesthetic sensibilities of the parents or society. An abortion in these circumstances, says Dr. Kenneth J. Ryan, Professor of Obstetrics and Gynecology and Chairman of the Department of Obstetrics and Gynecology at Western Reserve University, "in fact is done for the family and society."

Although some parents and physicians have indicated a desire to abort out of compassion for the child who would bear these defects, this is a difficult moral line to follow. People ask, "How would you like to be

[26]*Life,* June 4, 1965.

born deformed?" The child might reply, "If it is a choice of that or no life at all, I might choose life."[27]

Some, in fact, have actually declared this to be their choice. During the debate in Great Britain over liberalization of that country's abortion law, a letter was published in the *Daily Telegraph* from three residents of an institution for the crippled. It read:

Sir—We were disabled from causes other than thalidomide, the first of us having two useless arms and hands, the second two useless legs, and the third the use of neither arms nor legs.

We are fortunate only, it may seem, in having been allowed to live, and we want to say with strong conviction how thankful we are that no one took it upon themselves to destroy us as useless cripples. Here, in the Thomas Delarue School for Spastics . . . we have found worthwhile and happy lives and we face our future with confidence. Despite our disabilities life still has much to offer, and we are more than anxious—if only metaphorically—to reach out towards the future.[28]

ON THE LEGAL FRONT

Coinciding with such dramatic and well-publicized events as the thalidomide tragedy and the rubella epidemic, support for relaxation of the laws came from a recommendation of the influential American Law Institute for new Model Penal Code sections on abortion. The proposed law, described by a critic

[27]Ryan in Smith, 66.
[28]Parliamentary Debates, House of Commons, 1128.

as a "violent departure from all existing laws" on the subject,[29] states that a licensed physician is "justified" in terminating pregnancy: (1) if he believes there is "substantial risk" that continuance of the pregnancy would "gravely impair the physical or mental health" of the mother, or that the child would be born with grave mental or physical defect, or if the pregnancy results from rape or incest; and (2) if two physicians, one of whom may be the physician performing the operation, certify in writing their "belief" in the "justifying" circumstances. The ALI proposal or some variation of it has been the basis of the efforts to enact liberalized abortion laws in more than twenty states at this writing.

Despite the zealous support mustered for the several bills based on the ALI statute, many of its most ardent backers concede that they do not regard it as the final word on the subject but rather as hardly more than the opening shot in a long-term battle. This certainly is the position of those pro-abortion forces cited above who see the ultimate solution not in more liberal laws but in no laws at all. Writes Lawrence Lader:

> The complete legalization of abortion is the one just and inevitable answer to the quest for feminine freedom. All other solutions are compromises. The American Law Institute Code offers a practical plan that might eventually be accepted by a few state legis-

[29]Eugene Quay, "Justifiable Abortion," *The Georgetown Law Journal,* Vol. 49, No. 2 (Winter, 1960), 173-256; Vol. 49, No. 3 (Spring, 1961), 395-538. Page 173.

latures. But it evades the real problem, touching only a fraction of essential cases, and leaving the average woman chained to a tenuous and possibly unmanageable law, and the medical profession still struggling to decide what cases can be accepted under the vague definition of "health."[30]

In view of this profession of relative *sangfroid* on the subject of the ALI proposal, it is somewhat surprising to find Mr. Lader denouncing the "shame and irresponsibility of our legislatures" after the New York State Assembly's Codes Committee in March, 1967, rejected a similar bill to liberalize that state's abortion law. Mr. Lader pledged at the same time to help organize a "counseling service in abortion," and said it would make "necessary medical services" available to "any woman in need."[31]

Other writers also speak of passage of the ALI statute or legislation based on it as no more than an opening wedge in an ongoing effort. Having remarked that "we shall scarcely have helped many women" by obtaining passage of a liberalized law, Alice S. Rossi, a research associate with the Committee on Human Development of the University of Chicago, says: "Any woman, whether married or not, should be able to secure a safe abortion, upon her own request, at a reasonable fee, in a licensed hospital by a licensed and competent physician."[32]

[30]Lader, 169.
[31]*New York Times*, March 12, 1967.
[32]Alice S. Rossi, "Abortion Laws and Their Victims," *Trans-action*, September/October, 1966.

Elsewhere, in a notable exposition of strategy for pro-abortion forces, she describes passage of a reform statute along the lines of the ALI version as "only one step on the way to the goal of maximum individual freedom for men and women to control their own reproductive lives. Such freedom should include the personal right to undo a contraceptive failure by means of a therapeutic abortion. . . ."[33] Dr. Harold Rosen concludes that "mature legal consideration of mother, family, children, and society would lead legislatures not to pass more liberalized abortion laws but to abolish such laws altogether."[34]

THE HEAT OF THE BATTLE

The prolonged and bitter conflict that took place over the effort to change this law (on abortion) was . . . unequaled. . . . The subject was that topic of "many ardent debates" in the medical societies, and it is evident that the liberal journals and newspapers of the period were full of proposals for revisions and of discussions supporting various points of view. The whole problem became a political issue, and the agitation reached the point where mass meetings were held; and books, novels, and plays were based upon the theme.[35]

So contemporary a ring does the above passage have that it could serve with a few exceptions—so

[33]Alice S. Rossi, "Public Views on Abortion," Committee on Human Development, University of Chicago, February, 1966.

[34]Rosen in Smith, 105.

[35]Paul H. Gebhard, Wardell B. Pomeroy, Clyde E. Martin, Cornelia V. Christenson, *Pregnancy, Birth and Abortion* (New York, 1958), p. 237.

far we have been spared many novelized and dramatized treatments of the abortion issue—as a description of the debate now raging throughout the United
States. Actually, however, the passage describes, not
the contemporary American scene, but the situation
in Germany early in this century when a similar battle
was being waged. Abortion, it appears, is always an
emotional issue. It is probably asking too much to
hope for a calm discussion on the merits of the case,
but what is still more discouraging is that it is apparently asking too much even to request that the
debate be conducted without vituperation and bit-
terness. Thus it is disheartening but not particularly
surprising to find a critic of the Catholic Church's
stand on abortion deploring the "rigidity" of the
Church and writing, "I cannot but marvel at this
Church's tenacity in applying the ambiguities of
antiquity to the clear-cut issues of today."[36] Nor is it
surprising to find a clergyman scoring "medieval-
minded laymen and clerics" for their opposition to
abortion.[37] On this issue most of the ordinary cour-
tesies of debate—to say nothing of dialogue—seem
to be automatically discarded.

One writer traces the start of pressure for relax-

[36]Hall in Smith, 231-32. Dr. Hall is president of the Association for the Study of Abortion. His essay appears as a
closing "commentary" on a series of articles analyzing the
pros and cons of abortion. It is difficult to fathom the edi-
torial objectivity which gives the final, judgmental word in
such a collection to an active proponent of legalized abortion.
[37]Rabbi William F. Rosenblum, quoted in *The New York
Times,* February 12, 1967.

ation of the abortion laws to 1955, when the Planned Parenthood Federation of America sponsored a three-day conference on abortion which was attended by specialists in medicine, psychiatry, law, sociology and other fields.[38] It was not until the early nineteen-sixties, however, following the adoption by the American Law Institute of its proposed code, that actual legislation calling for easier abortion began to crop up in the legislatures of such states as California, New Hampshire, New York, Illinois and Kansas. And it was not until 1967 that the issue became a matter of legislative urgency throughout the nation, and the first "reform" statutes were, as already noted, enacted in Colorado, North Carolina and California.

Probably the bitterest and certainly the most widely publicized of the legislative fights of that year was waged in New York, where bills to relax that state's abortion law—permitting termination of pregnancy only to save the life of the mother—had previously been introduced in 1965 and 1966. The New York controversy rapidly took on a strongly denominational cast. On February 12, a pastoral letter—the first ever issued jointly by the bishops of the state's eight Catholic dioceses—was read at Masses in Catholic churches throughout the state. The pastoral said:

Dearly beloved in Christ:
The purpose of this joint pastoral letter is to invite your most serious reflection on our position as Catho-

[38]Rosen in Smith, 102.

lics regarding the right to life of every human being and our consequent opposition to abortion.

The right of innocent human beings to life is sacred and inviolable. It comes from God Himself. The Second Vatican Council, in its *Pastoral Constitution on the Church in the Modern World,* declared clearly the position of the Catholic Church regarding abortion.

"God," the Council says, "has conferred on man the surpassing ministry of safeguarding life—a ministry which must be fulfilled in a manner worthy of man. Therefore, from the moment of its conception, life must be guarded with the greatest care, while abortion and infanticide are unspeakable crimes."

Since laws which allow abortion violate the unborn child's God-given right, we are opposed to any proposal to extend them. We urge you most strongly to do all in your power to prevent direct attacks upon the lives of unborn children.

We are by no means blind to the sufferings of mothers and to the problems confronting some families. We shall always support every effort to alleviate human suffering and to solve personal and family problems, but we insist that any solution must respect the life of the innocent, defenseless, unborn child.

We earnestly hope that all who sincerely wish society to retain its humanity while solving human problems will join with us in defending the sanctity of the human right to life.[39]

Throughout the controversy in New York, opposition to the "reform" bill was, at least by proponents of the legislation, identified almost exclusively with the Catholic church. Some went even further and sought to identify the opposition simply with the

[39]The New York bishops were not alone in this. Joint pastorals have also been issued by the bishops of California and other states, as well as by many individual bishops.

Catholic bishops. *The New York Times,* for example, declared editorially that "The Roman Catholic hierarchy stands almost alone as a significant opposition force."[40] Earlier, however, the same newspaper, reporting an effort by unnamed persons to recruit support among prominent lay Catholics for relaxation of the law, stated that the effort had "met with failure" because no significant support for easier abortion could be found among Catholic lay leaders.[41] Following the appearance of the bishops' joint pastoral, a 1,000-word statement was issued jointly by the Protestant Council of the City of New York, the New York Federation of Reform Synagogues, the Association of Reform Rabbis and the New York Metropolitan Region of the United Synagogue of America in which the "harsh and unbending posture" of the Catholic Church in opposing abortion was criticized. The statement, released at a news conference, expressed hope "that better methods of communication than press conferences and pastoral letters may emerge for dialogue about our differences."[42] When the New York abortion bill was rejected in the state legislature—despite the endorsement of such prominent political figures as Governor Nelson Rockefeller, Senator Jacob Javits and Senator Robert Kennedy—a protest march was held in midtown Manhattan climaxed by picketing outside St.

[40]March 8, 1967.
[41]*The New York Times,* January 30, 1967.
[42]*The New York Times,* February 25, 1967.

Patrick's Cathedral. A pro-abortion spokesman stated, "I publicly accuse Cardinal Spellman and [Speaker of the State Assembly Anthony J.] Travia of being the executioners of the abortion law."[43]

The theme of much of the protest against opposition to the abortion bill was that it represented an effort by a minority (identified as Catholic) to thwart the will of the majority (identified as just about everybody else). Said *The New York Times:* "There are impressive moral arguments for and against abortion. But the Legislature should not continue to impose one moral view that cannot be reconciled with the needs and desires of so many citizens."[44] The difficulty with this is, of course, that it assumes that "the needs and desires of so many citizens" are the ultimate criteria of whether or not a measure should become law. This is a simplistic argument to say the least, for it means essentially that people should get whatever laws they want. But, as one writer has remarked, if the law "followed public practice only, the civil rights laws would never have been written."[45] The argument also ignores the fact that in a democracy parliamentary procedures and other techniques of supporting and opposing legislation are meant to be used—and constantly are *being* used by groups of every description on behalf of the ethical, economic, political and other positions

[43]*The New York Times,* March 13, 1967.
[44]*The New York Times,* February 27, 1967.
[45]Hellegers, "Law and the Common Good."

they espouse. There is no reason to expect or demand that opponents of easier abortion surrender this right. The current fight over abortion is after all being waged in the legislatures, and those who oppose abortion have as much right to fight there against it as those who favor it have to fight for it.

There is also reason to question the easy assumption that opposition to easier abortion is exclusively a Catholic stance. As a matter of fact, the proposals for "reform" legislation have been opposed by some Protestants, Orthodox Christians and Jews. But on a deeper level, identifying opposition to abortion as a "Catholic" position overlooks the fundamental issues involved. Denying that abortion is "a peculiarly Roman Catholic hang up," Pastor Richard John Neuhaus, a Lutheran clergyman and editor, has remarked that "the abortion debate touches upon our understanding of human life. Obviously, this is not an area of concern reserved by any religious grouping nor even, in any unique way, by religion as such. . . . The argument against abortion is not derived from church law but from a conviction regarding the prudent and just course for the whole of society."[46]

HOW MANY ABORTIONS?

Anybody who makes an attempt to examine the abortion issue objectively soon comes to realize that,

[46]Richard John Neuhaus, "The Dangerous Assumptions," *Commonweal*, June 30, 1967.

while hard facts on the extent of the problem are exceedingly difficult to come by, alleged "facts" about the incidence of abortion are in plentiful supply. Writers confidently offer figures on the total annual number of illegal abortions in the United States, although common sense alone would suggest that in the nature of things any such figures on an illegal practice must involve substantial guesswork. Dr. Robert Hall writes: "In the United States every year there are about four million births, one million spontaneous abortions, and one million induced abortions."[47] Other estimates put the number of induced abortions at a million and a half. Dr. Harold Rosen chooses a more dramatic method of presenting his figures, writing that "between ten and twenty criminal abortions are performed every fifteen minutes in this country. Estimates of twenty-five hundred per day are not unusual, and it may be a great deal more."[48] One writer, evidently of an economic turn of mind, speaks confidently of "the $350,000,000 annual intake of the abortion business."[49] How such figures are arrived at remains a mystery. It is a bit difficult to imagine either women who have undergone illegal abortions or doctors and others who have performed them reporting promptly to some central depository of statistics and providing as well information on the fee that was charged. One legis-

[47]Hall in Smith, 224.
[48]Rosen in Smith, 72-73.
[49]David Lowe, *Abortion and the Law* (New York, 1966), p. 77.

lator in Britain, where the habit of making unverified
and unverifiable assertions about the number of
abortions seems to be as common as in this country,
has remarked that "in the nature of the case there
can be no reliable statistics on the number of illegal
abortions . . . these statistics provided by parties to
the debate are so unreliable that they cannot be used
as a basis for a rational judgment."[50]

The various figures usually cited in debate over
abortion have as a matter of fact been subjected to
analysis. The results are intriguing in that they reflect what can only be called a highly unscientific
disregard for the facts and for scientific procedure.
Taking the frequently quoted figure of 1.2 million
illegal abortions annually in the United States, Dr.
Andre E. Hellegers notes that this estimate is based
on a 1934 study which drew its data from case histories given by 10,000 women who attended the
Margaret Sanger Birth Control Clinic in New York
between 1925 and 1929. "I leave it to your imagina-
tion," Dr. Hellegers has commented, "how representative that group must have been of the United
States in 1925. To give you some highlights, 45.1%
were foreign-born, 41.7% were Jewish and 26.1% were
Catholic (attending a birth control clinic in 1925-
1929). . . . I doubt that any first-year student in
an epidemiology course could get past the first se-
mester if he attempted to draw conclusions about the

[50]St. John-Stevas, *Parliamentary Debates*, 1154.

United States from a sample such as this."[51] Dr. Hellegers notes that, by using other studies as a starting point, one can obtain by extrapolation figures for the total number of U.S. illegal abortions each year that range from 600,000 to 100,000.

The matter is by no means a dry debate over numbers. Depending on whether one chooses to claim that there are 1.2 million illegal abortions in the United States each year or 100,000, one can argue either that abortion has already achieved de facto acceptance by a vast number of American women or that it is still practiced by a relatively small number. It is to the advantage of those who advocate relaxation of the abortion laws to claim as high a figure as possible, for, so the argument runs, if more than a million women are violating the existing laws each year, the laws are clearly unacceptable in the contemporary American social climate and should be changed. But the simple fact is that nobody really knows how many women have illegal abortions annually, and no reliable method has been developed to find out. Those who claim to have reliable—and astronomical—figures at hand are introducing a shabby debater's trick into what should be an objective discussion of a serious issue.

The same pattern appears in discussions of the

[51]Andre E. Hellegers, M.D., "A Doctor Looks at Abortion," in *Population Crisis,* hearings before the Subcommittee on Foreign Aid Expenditures of the Committee on Government Operations, United States Senate, Eighty-Ninth Congress, Second Session, Part 5-B (Washington, 1967), p. 1386.

number of deaths from illegal abortions. Once again it is to the advantage of the proponents of relaxed laws to set this figure high, since one of their arguments is that present laws force millions of women to undergo grave risk of life at the hands of quacks, criminals and perverts. It is therefore commonly said that 10,000 American women lose their lives each year as a result of illegal abortions. Of this figure Dr. Hellegers has written that "one can say, unequivocally and without fear of contradiction, that it is absurd."[52] It is, he notes, based on death rates given in a book published in 1936 by Dr. Frederick Taussig. Taussig, he points out, arrived at his figure by combining the abortion figure drawn from the Sanger Clinic case histories mentioned earlier with estimates of abortion incidence given by eighty-one doctors with rural practices, then applying a guessed-at mortality rate derived from a dubious German study, and, having by this round about route arrived at a figure of 8,000 abortion deaths, concluding magisterially that 10,000 is "nearer the truth." Remarks Dr. Hellegers: "If this study was a wonder in itself, it is even more remarkable that the figures are still being bandied about."

Along with statistical guesswork, the advocates of liberalized abortion laws also dwell on the incompetence and personal degradation of the illegal abortionists. Horror stories involving alcoholic doctors barred from practice and sexual degenerates abound

[52]Hellegers, 1388.

in the literature on the subject.[53] It is therefore somewhat surprising to find researchers with the Institute
for Sex Research speaking of the "technical ability
and the low number of deaths and ill effects resulting
from" the activities of illegal abortionists whom they
interviewed.[54] Dr. Hall—who states that the figure
of 5,000 to 10,000 abortion deaths yearly is "certainly" not correct and that the total number is
probably no more than 500—comments: "Even the
'unskilled' abortionist is evidently more skillful and/
or more careful these days than when Taussig com-
piled his figures."[55] And Dr. Rosen takes some of the
steaminess out of the horror stories when he remarks
matter-of-factly: "Eighty to ninety percent of all
abortions in the United States are performed by
competent physicians, on referral from other physicians."[56] The ghastly tales of the quack abortionists—"often virtual butchers,"[57] as Lawrence Lader
says of them—do make titillating and sensational
reading. But when even the advocates of easier abortion concede that most abortions are presently performed by qualified physicians the relevance of the
horror stories seems somewhat questionable.

ENDING ILLEGAL ABORTIONS

Nevertheless the argument persists that relaxed abor-

[53]See, e.g., Lowe, 19-39.
[54]Gebhard et al., 198.
[55]Hall in Smith, 228.
[56]Rosen in Smith, 73.
[57]Lader, 3.

tion laws are necessary in order to put the charlatan illegal abortionists out of business. (This argument, it might be remarked, is rather like saying that the best way of getting rid of bank robbers is to make it legal for everyone to hold up banks.) It is therefore of some significance to note that in countries which have legalized abortion, the illegal abortion rate has either remained the same or has risen. For instance, in the twelve years after Denmark enacted a liberalized abortion law in 1939 the number of legal abortions rose to 5,000 a year, while the number of illegal abortions rose to 9,000 a year.[58]

Even sponsors of legislation based on the American Law Institute statute concede that passage of the measure will have no impact on the great mass of abortions which are presently performed outside the law. Anthony G. Bielenson, a member of the California state assembly and one of the leading figures in the legislative drive there, acknowledged that enactment of the bill would have "absolutely no effect on the great majority of abortions which are now being illegally performed in California."[59] Despite this, the proponents of liberalization habitually cite the previously mentioned astronomical and undemonstrable guesses on the total number of abortions, as if the proposed legislation were actually related to these cases. Commenting on this, Dr.

[58]Quay, 439. This point will be examined in more detail below.
[59]Assemblyman Anthony G. Bielenson, quoted in Lowe, 86.

Hellegers has remarked: "If there are today about 10,000 therapeutic abortions performed yearly under the present laws, and if the changes in the law are, indeed, proposed to conform to present *medical* practice, then I daresay an extra thousand or so abortions may well be performed under the new law. But let no one in his right mind think that this has anything to do with the 1,200,000 other abortions [claimed by proponents of reform]."[60] Writes Alice Rossi: "If we rest content with goals limited to the penal code revision that is most likely to be passed, we shall scarcely have helped many women in the United States. Nor will such passage of a revised code be followed by any significant increase in legal abortions and decrease in illegal abortions, since the law will not cover most of the women who now have abortions illegally, i.e., married women who simply do not want any more children and use abortion as a birth control technique."[61]

What, then, is passage of these laws meant to accomplish? The answer is that it will help to condition legislatures to enactment of still more liberal legislation in the years to come and will help condition the public at large to the idea that abortion is socially acceptable. The ALI proposal is regarded by its strongest advocates as the camel's nose, opening the way for even more permissive public attitudes and legislation in the future. One way in which this

[60]Hellegers, "A Doctor Looks at Abortion," 1386.
[61]Rossi, "Abortion Laws and Their Victims."

could come about has been outlined by pro-abortion attorneys William Kopit and Harriet F. Pilpel. Were the ALI proposal to be enacted in New York, they suggest, it might be possible to give "a broad interpretation to the language of the statute so as to include every variety of economic and mental ill within the rubric of 'endangering the health of the mother.' That this result is possible cannot be questioned, especially if reputable physicians can be convinced to adopt the expansive construction. . . ."[62] Liberal interpretation of a statute based on the ALI proposal is, however, simply one means to the ultimate objective. As Alice Rossi has said, "passage of some version of the ALI recommendation . . . is only one step on the way to the goal of maximum individual freedom for men and women to control their own reproductive lives."[63] What this "control" means in practice is evident from her later statement that "women should have the same freedom to terminate an unwanted pregnancy as they have to use contraceptives to avoid pregnancy."[64]

PUBLIC ATTITUDES TOWARD ABORTION

In view of this it is pertinent to ask how people really feel about abortion. Realistically speaking, if the American public is in favor of abortion on demand, one can assume that that is what it will get, and op-

[62]William Kopit and Harriet F. Pilpel, "Abortion and the New York Penal Laws," memorandum.
[63]Rossi, "Public Views on Abortion."
[64]*Ibid.*

ponents of relaxing the abortion laws might as well cease their opposition now. If, on the other hand, the public is opposed to abortion or is prepared to tolerate it only in certain special circumstances, then it is well worth the effort to point out to the public that the long-range objectives of the abortion "reform" forces go much further than is customarily admitted.

How do people feel about abortion? In December, 1965, the National Opinion Research Center at the University of Chicago questioned a representative sample of 1,484 adult Americans on this point. It asked this question: "Please tell me whether or not you think it should be possible for a pregnant woman to obtain a legal abortion. . . ." There followed six suggested circumstances. The circumstances and the percentages of yes, no and don't know replies were as follows:[65]

"If the woman's own health is seriously endangered by the pregnancy": yes, 71%; no, 26%; don't know, 3%.

"If she became pregnant as a result of rape": yes, 56%; no, 38%; don't know, 6%.

"If there is a strong chance of serious defect in the baby": yes, 55%; no, 41%; don't know, 4%.

"If the family has a very low income and cannot afford any more children": yes, 21%; no, 77%; don't know, 2%.

"If she is not married and does not want to marry the man": yes, 18%; no, 80%; don't know, 2%.

[65]Rossi, "Abortion Laws and Their Victims."

"If she is married and does not want any more children": yes, 15%; no, 83%; don't know, 2%.

What this means, as Alice Rossi has remarked, is that "any suggestion of abortion as a last-resort means of birth control," the situation represented in the last three cases covered by the study, "is firmly rejected by the majority of American adults in the NORC sample."[66] Yet it is precisely these situations which the strongest supporters of abortion liberalization hope eventually to encompass, despite their constant emphasis on such extraordinary cases as rape and incest, fetal deformities and the rest. Their aim is to achieve the complete legalization of abortion as, in Lawrence Lader's phrase, "the final freedom,"[67] and thus to bring about legal recognition of what Kopit and Pilpel call the "utilitarian" principle that "no person has an absolute right to life."[68]

People who are trying to make up their minds about abortion, and, in particular, about the proposals to liberalize abortion laws, should consider this seriously. The liberalization proposals now pending strike many people as reasonable. They deal with extreme cases: rape, deformity and the rest, which play strongly on anyone's sympathies. No one, however, should suppose that if these proposals are enacted into law that will be the end of the matter. Their strongest supporters have assured us that it

[66]*Ibid.*
[67]Lader, 167 ff.
[68]Kopit and Pilpel, "Abortion and the New York Penal Laws."

will not be, and that nothing less than absolute freedom of abortion for everyone in every situation will satisfy them. We ought to take them at their word, for they are perfectly serious.

Iceland is a very small country, not much noted for contributions to the world's political or cultural scene. But Iceland was one of the pioneers among nations in enacting a liberalized abortion law, having done so in 1934. One of the leaders in this movement was Vilm Jónsson, at that time the country's chief medical officer. Jónsson was originally an advocate of abortion on "social" grounds. Within a few years, however, he had changed his mind. He explained why in an article written in 1937, and his words are well worth pondering in the light of the current controversy in the United States over "liberalization" of the law on abortion:

> While working and considering the matter in every bearing, I came to the conclusion that estimates of social indications would be so difficult, at least under conditions like those of my country, that the alternative was, in fact, not between medical indications on one side and medical indications plus social indications on the other, but between medical indications and no restrictions at all, with the consequence that any woman could have her fetus destroyed whenever she desired. I do not think that any responsible person would consider this desirable or even practicable.[69]

Whether they are "responsible" or not, this is

[69]Vilm Jónsson, quoted in Gebhard et al., 230.

precisely the course which is being loudly and per-
sistently advocated by some of the most active
proponents of "liberalized" abortion laws in the
United States today.

II

Abortion and Law

The American Declaration of Independence states:
"We hold these truths to be self-evident, that all men
are created equal, that they are endowed by their
Creator with certain inalienable Rights, that among
these are Life, Liberty and the pursuit of Happiness."
The Universal Declaration of Human Rights, proclaimed in December, 1948, by the United Nations
General Assembly, acknowledges in its preamble the
"equal and inalienable rights of all members of the
human family." Among the rights specifically defined
are those to "life, liberty, and security of person."

Nevertheless, even before the enactment of the first
"liberalized" abortion laws in 1967, abortion—the
direct taking of innocent life—was already permitted
under certain circumstances in every state in the
Union. In forty-five states abortions could be performed to save the life of the mother. In Alabama,
Oregon and the District of Columbia, abortions could
be performed to protect the mother's health. Colorado and New Mexico permitted abortion to "prevent
serious and permanent bodily injury." And in
Maryland such operations were legal when done in
order to "secure the safety of the mother." It can be

argued that pressure to relax the law still further was logical, if not necessarily inevitable, in view of these already substantial concessions. For if innocent life may legally be attacked directly in one case, it is at best difficult to argue convincingly that it may not be attacked in another.

The first state to adopt a law dealing directly with abortion was Connecticut, which did so in 1821. Over the next twenty years a number of other states followed suit. The legislation enacted during this period has been summarized as follows:

> Most of the early American statutes dealt severely with abortions performed after quickening [the stage of pregnancy at which the movements of the fetus are felt for the first time], but were relatively quite lenient as to abortions at an earlier stage. Most of them began with rather loose authorization of abortions based on the opinions of one or two medical men that they were necessary to preserve the life of the mother, but a few years' experience generally brought amendments to limit exemptions to cases in which the abortion *was* necessary, with no substitution of a physician's declared opinion for the fact.[1]

In general, the statutes forbade direct abortion or attempts to bring it about, unless necessary to preserve the life of the mother. English penal laws by contrast made no such exception. Legislative sanction of abortion to save the life of the mother is an American contribution.

[1]Eugene Quay, "Justifiable Abortion," *The Georgetown Law Journal*, Vol. 49, No. 2 (Winter, 1960), 173-256; Vol. 49, No. 3 (Spring, 1961), 395-538. Page 437.

Since the controversy over easing restrictions on abortion is often presented as a struggle by the rest of the community against the intransigence of the Roman Catholic Church, it is significant that the first American laws against abortion were enacted in a time and place in which Catholics were "an object of curiosity rather than a political force."[2] However changes in social mores may have altered matters, the adoption of these American statutes during the first half of the nineteenth century testifies to a rejection of abortion, except when necessary to save the mother's life, that was very far from being an exclusively Roman Catholic position. It is also beside the point to attack abortion laws because of the presumed sexual and religious attitudes of more than a century ago—attitudes described as being hypocritical, antisexual, neurotically puritan. As a Lutheran writer has remarked in commenting on this point: "The validity of a law is not dependent upon its origins but upon its present function. A law which may have been established for the wrong reasons in the last century may be supported for different and more humane reasons today."[3] Furthermore it is something less than fair to adopt the tactic of some proponents of liberalized abortion laws who first impute bad—hypothetical—motives to the men who enacted these laws in the nineteenth century and then

[2]Quay, 445.
[3]Richard John Neuhaus, "The Dangerous Assumptions," *Commonweal*, June 30, 1967.

assign the same—equally hypothetical—motives to those who oppose their repeal today.

One need not, after all, be an antisexual puritan to conclude that strict laws against abortion are in the best interests of society. A Church of England group which studied the question exhaustively lists three "interests" which are served by such laws—interests which have nothing to do with the gratification of neurotic drives but relate rather to the well-being of society.[4] The first of these is "the right to life itself, as a right belonging to every human being who does not forfeit it by his own unlawful act." This is a consideration of great importance for the professions of medicine and law—medicine because of its commitment to preserving human life, law because of its commitment to protecting human rights. The second interest is "the interest of society in its own life and survival." As will be seen below, abortion can be a threat to maternal health and, on a broad demographic scale, can cause serious population imbalances with dangerous long-range implications for the economic and social health of a nation. The third interest is "the interest of society in maintaining its witness that some acts are morally reprobate within that society." This, it should be noted, is not the same thing as saying that every element of private morality should be enacted into law; although it should be

[4]*Abortion, An Ethical Discussion,* published for the Church Assembly Board for Social Responsibility by the Church Information Office (London, 1965), pp. 18-21.

recognized at the same time that every law embodies *somebody's* morality. Rather, as the British church group put it: "The interest maintained by this third element in the legal tradition . . . is society's interest in humanity itself, in the very high value placed upon persons, who are de-valued equally in loose and irresponsible attitudes to sexual relationship and in a light regard for unborn and infant life."

Since British law has obviously played a major role in shaping American law and since, in any event, the British legal experience is constantly cited in the abortion debate, it is well worth spending some time to see what this experience has been.

Abortion was definitely recognized as a crime in common law. Coke and Blackstone describe it as "a great misprision," "a heinous offence." In their treatment of the crime, however, the common law jurists took over the distinction, present also in canon law, between the fetus before quickening and after quickening. Said Blackstone: "Life begins in contemplation of law as soon as an infant is able to stir in the mother's womb." The distinction is apparent, too, in his interpretation of the common law tradition that a pregnant woman could not be hanged. This would hold true, he said, only if the woman was "quick with child—for barely with child, unless he be alive in the womb, is not sufficient."

The first modern law against abortion in England was enacted in 1803—by a Parliament in which no Catholic sat. For the past century, however, the main law has been the Offences Against the Person Act of 1861. It provided for punishment by life imprisonment of any person who deliberately caused a woman to miscarry, or any woman who employed means to cause her own miscarriage, the actions being defined as felonies. One who knowingly supplied drugs or instruments for an abortion committed a misdemeanor which could be punished by up to five years in prison.

THE BOURNE CASE AND AFTER

The legal situation in England was, however, changed significantly as a result of the case of *Rex v. Bourne* in 1938. If anyone may claim the title of patron saint of the movement for easier abortion, it is surely Dr. Aleck Bourne. Dr. Bourne, an obstetric surgeon, performed an abortion on a fourteen-year-old girl who was pregnant as a result of having been raped by soldiers. He acted with the consent of the girl and her father, and performed the operation in a hospital. It is usually said that Dr. Bourne then notified the police of what he had done—presumably in order to provoke a test case. In fact, however, it appears that the incident actually came to the attention of the authorities through a letter probably sent by one of the British abortion law reformers of the day.[5] When confronted by the police, Dr. Bourne readily admitted what he had done and asked to be arrested.

[5]Paul Ferris, *The Nameless: Abortion in Britain Today* (London, 1966), p. 46.

He was charged with violating the Offences Against the Person Act and tried.

Easily the most noteworthy feature of the trial was the instruction to the jury by Judge Macnaghten. The judge began by contrasting Dr. Bourne's case with the ordinary criminal abortion case to come to trial in which the operation was performed furtively by an untrained individual acting for money. By contrast, he said, Dr. Bourne was "a man of the highest skill," who had performed an abortion "as an act of charity, without fee or reward, and un-questionably believing that he was doing the right thing." The judge did not indicate how Dr. Bourne's altruism was related to the legal question.

Judge Macnaghten then went on to define the heart of the issue. "The question that you have got to determine," he told the jurors, "is whether the Crown has proved to your satisfaction beyond reason-able doubt that the act which Dr. Bourne admittedly did was not done in good faith for the purpose only of preserving the life of the girl." The key phrase here, it soon developed, was "preserving . . . life." The law permitted abortion "for the preservation of the life of the mother." What did this mean? "I do not think," Judge Macnaghten instructed the jurors, "that it is contended that those words mean merely for the preservation of the life of the mother from instant death." On the contrary, urging the jury to take a "reasonable" view of the words of the law, the judge said: "If the doctor is of opinion, on reasonable

grounds and with adequate knowledge, that the probable consequence of the continuance of the pregnancy will be to make the woman a physical or
mental wreck, the jury is quite entitled to take the
view that the doctor, who, in those circumstances,
and in that honest belief, operates, is operating for
the purpose of preserving the life of the woman."
The jury, needless to say, voted for acquittal.[6]

Judge Macnaghten's instructions have had a pro-
found effect on subsequent legal and extralegal discussions of abortion. Under his interpretation, a doctor who could convince a jury of his reasonable belief
that a particular pregnancy would make a woman
"a physical or mental wreck" could not be convicted
of the crime of abortion. Advocates of easier abortion have acclaimed the judge's reasoning as mark-
ing "a new epoch in our law."[7] More recently a
member of the British House of Lords has commented: "Mr. Justice Macnaghten found what he
deemed to be a loophole in the law. He widened
it to a breach, and subsequent cases have widened
the breach still further, so that any of your Lord-
ships could drive through it a horse and cart or
an abortionist in his limousine."[8]

The influence of the Macnaghten views soon be-

[6]The text of Justice Macnaghten's direction to the jury
is contained in Quay, 521-526.

[7]Quay, 433.

[8]Lord Craigmyle in Parliamentary Debates (Hansard),
House of Lords, Vol. 270, No. 11 (November 30, 1965),
1222.

came apparent in British judicial rulings. In *Rex v. Bergmann and Ferguson* (1948) a judge held that the question was not whether the abortion was "in fact" necessary but whether the doctor "believed" it was; if the latter, it was legal. In *Regina v. Newton and Stungo* (1958) the judge held that abortion was permitted to preserve the life or health of the mother, and he specifically included mental health. The post-*Bourne* situation was summed up by one writer in these words: "Since that time, it appears to be generally accepted that if a doctor procures an abortion because he believes it is in the interest of the physical or psychological health of the mother, no action will be taken against him by the law."[9]

Nevertheless the situation did not satisfy abortion law reformers, who insisted instead on statutory guarantees. Beginning in 1954, when a liberalized abortion bill was introduced in the House of Lords, persistent efforts were made to enact legislation permitting easier abortion. In 1967 these efforts were crowned with success. Despite widespread public controversy a liberalization bill was enacted in July by the House of Commons. In October it was accepted by the House of Lords.

The legislation provides that a doctor may legally perform an abortion with the concurrence of a second physician. Grounds for the operation include the risk of injury to the physical or mental health of the

[9]John Marshall, M.D., *Medicine and Morals* (Glen Rock, New Jersey, 1964), p. 67. Deus Books edition.

woman "or any existing children of her family." The latter provision clearly relates to the so-called "social" indications for abortion, such as possible housing or educational problems; it has no connection with medical indications for abortion. In making this determination the doctors may take into consideration the woman's "total environment, actual or reasonably foreseeable." Abortions may also be performed where there is risk that the child will be born with serious mental or physical abnormalities, where the mother is mentally defective, where the pregnancy results from rape, or where the mother is under sixteen.

Commenting on the provision for abortion where the child may be defective, one observer has described this as "an important new departure in the law. Sacrificing the life of the foetus to protect the mother is one thing; depriving it of life because of a prognostication of abnormality is quite different. For one thing, how can 'likely' be sufficiently certainly established in the present state of medical knowledge? . . . It would indeed be far more reasonable to wait unto the child was born and then dispatch it if it was found to be deformed." In addition, this provision "pre-supposes that one human being can make a judgment about another as to whether that other's life is worth living and enforce it, a power that has never been conferred by Anglo-American law. It confers a license to kill and one with no clear limiting terms. . . . Instead of the clear standard of the law there is substituted the subjective canon of personal taste."[10]

Although there was strong Catholic opposition to the British "reform" bill, Catholics were by no means the only ones fighting the measure. One particularly active group was an organization known as the Society for the Protection of the Unborn Child, which had a strong representation of physicians and other professional people among its members and did not include any Catholics on its executive board.[11] The society conducted a large-scale campaign to secure signatures for a petition to Prime Minister Harold Wilson opposing the reform bill. The petition read:

> We, the undersigned, while accepting the need for a moderate measure of abortion law reform, believe that the proposals in the present Termination of Pregnancy Bill threaten the principle of sanctity of human life long implicit in our law. In view of the vital importance to the community of soundly-based legislation we urge Her Majesty's Government to set up a royal commission to investigate and establish all the relevant facts.

Pressure for legislative action, however, in the end swamped requests for study of the facts. During debate in the House of Lords, Archbishop Michael Ramsey, Primate of the Church of England, while declaring that he would support a bill which made

[10]Norman St. John-Stevas, "Abortion Laws," *Commonweal*, November 11, 1966.

[11]National Catholic News Service, March 14, 1967.

risk to the life of the mother the sole ground for abortion, criticized the pending legislation because of "some particularly bad features" in it. In particular, he said, the measure ran counter to the principle "that the human fetus is sacred and has a right to live and develop."[12]

The British bill, however, like other legislation to make abortions easier to obtain, starts from the premise that the life of the unborn child is *not* sacred and may be destroyed if society or the parents so wish. This is, to say the least, a departure from legal tradition. As Norman St. John-Stevas has remarked:

> The notion of the sanctity of life is implicit in the common law idea of man as *liber et legalis homo:* it becomes explicit in the great series of declarations of the rights of man from the American revolution down to our own day. Rooted in the Christian notion of man as a creature destined for eternal life, it is reinforced today by modern man's psychological awareness of his own uniqueness. The acceptance of this concept by our law has made a profound difference to our society. It is the premise not only of liberty but also of equality and fraternity.[13]

THE MODEL PENAL CODE

The sections on abortion in the Model Penal Code recommended by the American Law Institute are as follows:

[12]National Catholic News Service, July 25, 1967.
[13]St. John-Stevas, "Abortion Laws."

Section 207.11. Abortion and Related Offenses.

(1) *Unjustified Abortion.* A person who purposely and unjustifiably terminates the pregnancy of another otherwise than by a live birth commits a felony of the third degree or, where the pregnancy has continued beyond the twenty-sixth week, a felony of the second degree.

(2) *Justifiable Abortion.* A licensed physician is justified in terminating pregnancy if:

(a) he believes there is substantial risk that continuance of the pregnancy would gravely impair the physical or mental health of the mother or that the child would be born with grave physical or mental defect, or the pregnancy resulted from rape by force or its equivalent as defined in Section 207.4(1) or from incest as defined in Section 207.3; and

(b) two physicians, one of whom may be the person performing the abortion, have certified in writing their belief in the justifying circumstances, and have filed such certificate prior to the abortion in the licensed hospital where it was to be performed, or in such other place as may be designated by law.

Substantial attacks have been launched against this proposed statute and others modeled on it. The critics advance a number of arguments: that the statute is seriously deficient in defining its key terms; that it does not provide adequate safeguards to keep unscrupulous doctors from performing abortions on trivial grounds; that it violates the unborn child's right to due process and equal protection of the laws in a number of particulars; and that it would tend to appear as a "vindication" of abortion to the many people for whom the fact that something is "legal" automatically means that it is also "moral." In more detail, the legal and constitutional objections raised against the proposed statute include the following: [14]

1. *Failure to define terms.* The proposed statute does not explain what it understands by "gravely" in the phrase "gravely impair the physical or mental health of the mother," nor does it say what it understands by "grave" in the phrase "grave physical or mental defect." It would thus leave excessive discretion to individual doctors in what is literally a matter of life and death. Every pregnancy could be considered a threat to the mother's health or life if one wished to stretch a point (and proponents of easier abortion through liberalized interpretation of the law do). Under the proposed statute, a physician who wished to take this view would be legally "justified" in terminating any pregnancy by abortion.

"Substantial risk" is another term for which no definition is given. How would the determination of substantial risk be made? If on a statistical basis, what percentage of mortality and morbidity would be considered substantial? But since statistics can only be applied in general and not to specific cases,

[14]The analysis that follows is for the most part drawn from Quay, 174-180, and 439-446, and two position papers prepared by Vaughan, Brandlin, Robinson & Roemer of Los Angeles, as attorneys for the Southern California Conference of Catholic Charities, in opposition to abortion bills in the California legislature.

how could statistics ever properly be the basis for deciding whether *this particular* unborn child should live or die? Also, in determining whether a substantial risk is involved in a particular case, a doctor must make an individual judgment based on his observation of that particular patient. Supposing his judgment is that her prospects are poor if the pregnancy continues, how poor must they be for the risk to be "substantial"? The Model Penal Code is silent on this point, leaving the decision—absolutely one of life or death so far as the unborn child is concerned—in the hands of just two men.

Also lacking in definition is the term "health," particularly "mental health." Here, too, the statute would give individual practitioners virtually unlimited leeway to perform abortions.

Some of course argue that in other areas of medical practice such matters are left to the discretion of the doctor and that this should be true of abortion also. But the framers of the American Law Institute statute and those who are pushing for its enactment have, by their involvement in the legislative battle, already conceded that abortion is a special case, where medical practice requires strict supervision by law, presumably because of the larger societal issues involved. If that is so, one cannot very well have it both ways, arguing that there is simultaneously need for a law but no need for strict legal definitions within the law. If the ALI statute or any other abortion law is necessary, sound legal practice demands that it make quite clear what is permitted and what is not under the law.

2. *Failure to protect against the unethical.* Medicine, like any profession, has a minority of unethical practitioners. The Model Penal Code, however, makes no distinction—if indeed any could be made workable in law—between these men and their reputable colleagues. Unpleasant as it is to contemplate, it is possible to envision situations in which greedy quacks would in effect put their power to sanction abortions up for sale to the highest bidders, without regard for whether the operations were actually "justified" even within the very elastic terms of the law. Paul Ferris, a British writer who is in favor of easier abortion, nevertheless concedes the existence of medical men who "let themselves be used as a social convenience because of the money."[15] There is no reason to suppose that the American medical profession is free of this questionable element.

The statute makes no requirement that the physician even conduct an examination of the woman. All he need do is certify a "belief" in the existence of circumstances justifying the abortion, without offering any substantiating proof that they do in fact exist. This "belief" requirement is altogether meaningless as it stands, since there is simply no way to disprove a physician's assertion that he "believed" abortion to be required, no matter how farfetched

[15]Ferris, 132.

the case may seem to an impartial observer. Proving the non-necessity of abortion is an "almost impossible burden" for a potential prosecutor, as one legal writer has noted;[16] proving the non-belief of the doctors in justifying circumstances is, one may assume, an absolute impossibility.

Nor need the two certifying doctors be specialists; in fact, neither need be an obstetrician or a psychiatrist, even though these represent the two areas of specialization with particular competence in cases involving the physical and mental health of mothers.

Further, the proposed statute fails to lay down any firm criteria for the hospitals in which abortions are to be performed, beyond specifying that they be "licensed." During the hearings in the California legislature on a proposal for easier abortion, fear was expressed that if abortions were permitted in very small hospitals, surveillance might be difficult and the result could be the creation of a number of "abortion mills."[17]

3. *Failure to safeguard the child.* Under our system of law, a person charged with a capital offense must be indicted, and the indictment must be tested for sufficiency. An attorney must be provided for a defendant who cannot afford his own, and the defendant must be given time to prepare his defense, must have the right to confront his accusers and

[16]B. James George, Jr., "Current Abortion Laws: Proposals and Movements for Reform," in David T. Smith, ed., *Abortion and the Law* (Cleveland, 1967), p. 25.

[17]National Catholic News Service, May 28, 1965.

must enjoy an open trial of which a record is made.
Thus at every step even the most serious offender
receives the most careful protection of the law to
ensure that his rights are not violated, and the least
hint of a miscarriage of justice is enough to send
shudders of concern through members of the legal
profession and the public at large. So far as the
Model Penal Code is concerned, however, the unborn child threatened with abortion, though he is
guilty of no crime and is charged with none, does
not enjoy such elementary protections as a defender,
a hearing, specifications to support the demand for
his destruction, and the right of appeal.

No State has the right to take innocent life. On
the contrary, all provide elaborate safeguards—and
rightly so—to prevent the execution of an innocent
person. The proposed statute, by contrast, would
permit the taking of the innocent life of an unborn
child virtually without safeguards. It is ironic that
pressure for easier abortion should be rising at a time
when many persons, prompted by religious or humanitarian considerations, advocate an end to capital
punishment even for the worst of criminals. It is
ironic, too, that this pressure should exist at precisely
the time when society's concern for better legal protection of children is growing. As the Dean of the
Boston College Law School has noted, interest in
laws against the physical abuse of children reflects
society's feeling of "a deep responsibility to protect
children even at the expense of restricting the right

to privacy enjoyed by married couples."[18] Logically there is no reason why this sense of responsibility should extend to the child who has been born, but not to the unborn child.

4. *Violation of due process and equal protection of the laws.* Although the unborn child is a person with an inalienable right to life, he could under the proposed statute be condemned to death in secret and summary proceedings and without representation. Some of course assert—it can only be an assertion—that the child does not become a "person" until some specified point in his development. But besides being unprovable in the nature of things and contrary to traditional law, ethics and medicine,[19] the point is irrelevant in this context because the statute itself sets no time limit within which the abortion must be performed. It can scarcely be maintained—although some have perversely sought to do so—that the child is not a person until after birth. Children born prematurely can and do survive, a fact which makes it clear beyond the possibility of dispute that, after a certain point at least, a child is capable of living outside his mother's body though ordinarily he would not be born until later. Some, of course, note that doctors generally advise against abortion after the twelfth week of pregnancy and consider this safeguard enough. If that is the case,

[18]Robert F. Drinan, S. J., "The Inviolability of the Right to be Born," in Smith, 118.
[19]See Marshall, 66.

they should be aware that the more ardent abortion proponents do not even consider the twelve-week limit sacrosanct. Dr. Harold Rosen, for example, has proclaimed that "any pregnancy . . . can be interrupted from the moment it has been diagnosed to the moment of spontaneous delivery. Physicians who maintain that an abortion cannot safely be performed after the twelfth week are either ten years behind in their knowledge of medical practice or are deliberately falsifying medical information to their patients."[20] However one may evaluate the substance of Doctor Rosen's statement, it is certainly worth consideration by those who think the law can safely be silent on the point beyond which abortion will not be permitted.

A minimum concept of due process demands that life should not be taken except for a proportionately grave cause. Existing laws, which permit abortion only when necessary to save the mother's life, at least weigh one life against another: an approach which, while morally inadmissible, does reflect an attempt in the direction of due process. Under the proposed statute, by contrast, innocent life could be taken for causes whose gravity is in no way comparable. Further, the statute would leave the determination of life or death to secret proceedings conducted by medical practitioners rather than judicial authorities. It would authorize these same

[20]Harold Rosen, M.D., "Psychiatric Implications of Abortion: A Case Study in Social Hypocrisy," in Smith, 96.

medical practitioners, men without legal training, to decide whether rape or incest had occurred—a question on which courts themselves would hesitate to claim infallible competence. There is no reason in good law, good medicine or good sense for such an arrangement.

Dr. Andre Hellegers has commented tellingly on the statute's provision for abortion in cases of rape. Presumably the reason for abortion in such cases is the otherwise intolerable mental strain on the mother, the argument in the *Bourne* case. If this is so, the law should at least require some indication of mental strain. Writes Dr. Hellegers:

> I suggest . . . that the minimum evidence of maternal strain could be a willingness to consult a physician within five days of the occurrence of rape. This would permit the performance of a uterine curettage *before implantation has occurred,* which is already legal and would have several advantages: It would be psychologically better not to know for certain that one had been impregnated by a rapist; it is less dangerous to curette a nonpregnant uterus; it would eliminate the well-known syndrome of the woman who "rapes awful easy," and would then like an abortion; it would also be easier to prosecute the rapist, if known, if early charges were pressed against him.[21]

This, it should be noted, is not an argument for abortion in cases of rape. It is rather a suggestion of one of the minimal provisions which should be

[21]Andre E. Hellegers, M.D., "Law and the Common Good," *Commonweal,* June 30, 1967.

included in any law which is going to permit abortion in rape cases. Such safeguards are lacking in the American Law Institute statute, which would make a woman's unsupported assertion that she had been raped grounds for destroying the life of an unborn child.

ARE UNBORN CHILDREN PERSONS?

If the unborn child is not a person in the eyes of the law, he can have no rights in the eyes of the law. This is not to suggest that the law can settle whether the unborn child is *in fact* a person or that the judgment of the law affects the fact one way or the other. The law must, however, make a determination in the matter for its own purposes, and its determination is obviously highly relevant in deciding whether proposed abortion liberalization statutes are consistent with legal doctrine.

It is therefore significant that the tendency in law —at least outside the area of abortion—is to recognize the unborn child as a person at all stages before birth. "The modern trend," one legal writer states, "is to recognize and embrace the medical fact that a child is a separate person from the moment of conception and to extend recovery to him for all injuries sustained by him from that time."[22] "With the exception of the abortion movement," another writer notes, "the universal trend in the law is

[22]Richard P. Byrne, "The Legal Rights of the Unborn Child," *Los Angeles Bar Bulletin,* November 1965.

toward full recognition of the humanity of the unborn child."[23]

This is seen in a number of ways. In Pennsylvania and New York, for instance, courts have held that a child may maintain a tort action after birth to recover for prenatal injuries, even though suffered very early in pregnancy.[24] In reaching this conclusion the Pennsylvania court quoted approvingly a New Jersey court's statement that "medical authorities have long recognized that a child is in existence from the moment of conception."[25] The New York court stated in part: "The complaint here, in alleging that plaintiff was in being in the third month of his mother's pregnancy alleges a conclusion of fact consistent with generally accepted knowledge of the process [of conception and human development]."

Even a century ago, a Pennsylvania court held to the same doctrine. It ruled in an abortion case that "the civil rights of an infant *in ventre sa mere* are fully protected at all periods after conception."[26] In 1949 an Ohio court held an unborn child to be a "person" within the meaning of the state constitu-

[23]Robert M. Byrn, "Abortion in Perspective," *Duquesne University Law Review*, Vol. 5, No. 2 (Winter 1966-1967).
[24]See *Sinkler v. Kneale*, 401 Pa. 267, 164 A.2d 93 (1960); *Kelly v. Gregory*, 282 App. Div. 542, 125 N.Y.S. 2d 696 (3d Dept. 1953); *Marko v. Philadelphia Trans. Co.*, 420 Pa. 124, 216 A.2d 502 (1966); *In re Bradley's Estate*, 50 Misc. 2d 72, 269 N.Y.S. 2d 657 (Surr. Ct., Nassau County, 1966).
[25]*Smith v. Brennan*, 31 N. J. 353, 362, 157 A.2d 497, 502 (1960).
[26]*Mills v. Commonwealth*, 13 Pa. 631, 633 (1850).

tion's guarantee of remedy by due course of law for an injury done to one in his person. The court stated:

> To hold that the plaintiff in the instant case did not suffer injury to her person would require this court to announce that as a matter of law, the infant is a part of the mother until birth and has no existence in law until that time. In our view such a ruling would deprive the infant of the right conferred by the Constitution upon all persons, by the application of a time-worn fiction not founded on fact and within common knowledge untrue and unjustified.[27]

One legal writer suggests that abortion is actually in conflict with the equal protection clause of the Fourteenth Amendment to the Constitution, much as legislative classification by race or color fails to stand the constitutional test because there is no "rational basis" for such classification. He states:

> . . . . [T] here is no qualitative difference, *scientifically speaking*, between human life in the womb and human life after birth. Hence, legislation, which would remove the life of a person in the womb from the full and equal protection of the law, would be as discriminatory, as "irrational," and as inimical to the equal protection clause as the legislative classification of races. Therefore, to [the] enumeration of persons under the aegis of the equal protection clause, we may now add "born or in the womb."[28]

One of the arguments frequently advanced by supporters of easier abortion laws is that such statutes

[27]152 Ohio St. 114, 87 N.E. 2d 334 (1949).
[28]Byrn, "Abortion in Perspective."

are merely "permissive" legislation and should not
be opposed. No one, it is said, is to be compelled to
undergo an abortion. How, then, can anyone presume
to interfere with those who do wish abortion? There
are several things to be said about this argument.
First, there is nothing very "permissive" about abortion from the unborn child's point of view. No one
consults him as to whether he agrees to this radical
infringement on his right to life. Second, the argument proves too much. It can be applied to too
many other situations. Presently there are laws which
restrict the speed at which motorists may drive.
Suppose some group of daredevil motorists began
demanding their repeal and argued that, after all,
they were not asking that others be *forced* to drive
at dangerous speeds but only that they be *allowed*
to do so, at least when they were convinced that
their doing so would not be a hazard to anyone
else. Would society therefore be obliged to give in to
their demands for "permissive" legislation that
abolished speed limits? Third, the argument ignores
the fact that most laws impose restrictions on somebody and in many cases on everybody. Restriction
is inherent in law, and sometimes law must even
cause suffering. But: "If the criterion for the legiti-
macy of laws were to be the complete absence of
'cruel' effects, we should abolish or drastically liberalize not only our abortion laws, but our statutes on
marriage, narcotics, homosexuality, suicide, eutha-

nasia, and numerous other laws which inevitably result in personal anguish from time to time."[29]

While it is true that laws which made it easier to obtain an abortion would not directly compel anyone to undergo such an operation, such laws would make it much easier for interested parties to exert private pressure to the same end. One can easily imagine chagrined husbands, worried lovers or anxious parents using the argument that "after all, it's legal" to force women into abortions. Nor should the educative impact of law be overlooked. Large numbers of people equate law with morality. "Permissive" laws on abortion would create an atmosphere of public acceptance for abortion. This of course is precisely what the most eager proponents of abortion want. There is, however, no reason to think that it is what the mass of the American people presently want. On the contrary, as the National Opinion Research Center study shows,[30] Americans do not want abortion to become part of the American way of life, except in certain limited cases, which are for the most part covered by existing law.

It is said that laws which are broken as often as those against abortion cannot be good laws and should be removed from the books. One writer asks: "Can a law which is violated a million times a year, and which would prosecute more than 2 million

[29]Rabbi Dr. Immanuel Jakobovits, "Jewish Views on Abortion," in Smith, 135.
[30]See above, pp. 38-39.

persons annually, be a good and just law?"[31] But the
evidence that the law is in fact violated "a million
times a year" is, as Dr. Hellegers has shown,[32]
flimsy to say the least. It would be a happy thing if
this particular figure could be dropped from the
abortion debate, or at least not used in an attempt
to score points. Furthermore, the argument can be
applied to other things besides abortion laws. Laws
against speeding are probably broken even more
than "a million times a year," but nobody seriously
suggests that this is a reason for striking them from
the books or enacting "permissive" laws which would
allow anyone to drive as fast as he liked. If the criterion of a good law were its observance, any law
could be discredited if enough people agreed to
violate it.

It is, of course, perfectly true that laws which
forbid abortion embody somebody's ideas on morality; so do laws which *permit* abortion; so for that
matter do all laws. But this is not the question. The
real question is not whether laws reflect someone's
idea of right and wrong, but whether they serve the
common good of society. Laws against abortion do.
Above all they protect the key societal principle that
innocent life may not be directly attacked—not on
grounds of convenience, nor relief of hardship, nor
even what appears to be necessity. "However con-

[31]David Lowe, *Abortion and the Law* (New York, 1966),
p. vii.
[32]See above, pp. 31-32.

venient, convincing, or compelling the arguments in favor of abortion may be," a legal scholar has written, "the fact remains that the taking of life, even though it is unborn, cuts out the very heart of the principle that *no one's* life, however unwanted and useless it may be, may be terminated in order to promote the health or happiness of another human being."[33] This surely is a principle whose protection is not only in the best interests of society but is essential to the continued existence of civilized society. As Pastor Richard John Neuhaus has remarked, "In our valuations of human life, to be civilized is to be conservative."[34]

[33]Drinan in Smith, 123.
[34]Neuhaus, "The Dangerous Assumptions."

III

Abortion and Medicine

Although most advocates of easier abortion now base their arguments on psychiatric or socioeconomic considerations—the idea that pregnancy is a threat to the mental health of the mother or that the birth of another child might overstrain the family's financial resources or otherwise upset its equilibrium—therapeutic abortion, one performed to promote or protect the physical health of the mother, still comes in for considerable discussion. In the past, furthermore, therapeutic abortion has been at the center of the debate. At one time or another a large number of physical conditions have been said to necessitate abortion. As recently as the nineteen-forties the New York Lying-In Hospital listed forty-four separate diseases and conditions of the mother as indications for therapeutic abortion.[1]

Several preliminary remarks deserve to be made. First and most obvious is that this is a very one-sided sort of therapy, with all the presumed benefit on the mother's side and none at all on the child's.

[1]Eugene Quay, "Justifiable Abortion," *The Georgetown Law Journal,* Vol. 49, No. 2 (Winter, 1960), 173-256; Vol. 49, No. 3 (Spring, 1961), 395-538. Page 183.

The infant mortality rate in abortions, it has been observed, is one hundred percent. Another factor apparent in the literature on this subject is the lack of agreement among medical writers. Many insist that abortion is necessary in certain circumstances, but few seem prepared to agree on what these are. It appears, too, that therapeutic abortion is a very elastic concept in the minds of its advocates. As Dr. Alan Guttmacher of Planned Parenthood has remarked:

> One of the difficulties about the problem of therapeutic abortion is the inequable distribution of the procedure. In borderline cases, and all too frequently in cases which are not even borderline, the patient's prestige and money are very vocal in getting an undesired pregnancy terminated. I am loath to admit it, but far too often a minor difficulty is stretched into a major abnormality for the right person.[2]

One point, however, on which there is universal agreement is that, as medical science has progressed, the medical argument for therapeutic abortion has faded to the vanishing point. A participant in a conference on abortion sponsored by the Planned Parenthood Federation of America stated, "There have been, even over so short a span of time as a decade, notable advances in therapeutics and management that have made many conditions formerly considered important medical indications for interruption of

[2]Quoted in a manuscript by John R. Cavanagh, M.D., *Abortion: Another Look*, p. 26.

pregnancy less valid, or have thrown them out entirely."[3] Another participant in the same conference put it even more strongly. "If we bring our entire therapeutic armament into operation," he said, "we can look after the somatic disorder whatever it may be."[4] There seems ample warrant for the conclusion of Dr. R. J. Heffernan of Tufts, who in 1951 told the Congress of the American College of Surgeons, "Anyone who performs a therapeutic abortion is either ignorant of modern medical methods of treating the complications of pregnancy or is unwilling to take time to use them."[5]

TUBERCULOSIS, HEART AND KIDNEY

It is beyond the scope of this study to review all the various diseases and physical conditions which at one time or another have been considered "indications" for therapeutic abortion and see how modern medical science has come to regard them. It may, however, be useful to consider how attitudes have changed toward the three conditions perhaps most frequently cited as justifying therapeutic abortion: tuberculosis, heart disease and kidney disease.

Tuberculosis. At the turn of the century it was commonly believed and taught that tuberculosis grew markedly worse in the course of pregnancy. Therefore it was common practice to abort a patient

[3]Mary Steichen Calderone, M.D., ed., *Abortion in the United States* (New York, 1958), pp. 87-88.
[4]Calderone, 108.
[5]Quoted in Quay, 184.

who showed any evidence of this disease. It may be questioned, however, whether even in this case abortion was purely a matter of therapy. "In fact," wrote Taussig in 1936, "the question of therapeutic abortion in tuberculosis of the lungs is intimately bound up with the social-economic status of the patient. In a poorly nourished woman with a large family, we must regard the saving of fetal life with less concern than in the woman who can and will carry out sanitorium treatment for the required period of time during and after her pregnancy, and for whom the saving of the child is a matter of great concern."[6]

Eventually, advances in treatment removed tuberculosis entirely as a serious indication for abortion. By 1958 an author was able to remark that "these patients [pregnant women with tuberculosis] get along as well or better than their nonpregnant sisters."[7] This was underlined in the same year by another writer, who stated, "Those qualified to render an opinion on the subject are skeptical of any good that may result from therapeutic interruption of pregnancy. Probably more women would be saved if greater care were given to the treatment of the tuberculosis and less attention paid to the complicating pregnancy."[8]

Heart disease. Heart disease was a common indi-

[6]Quoted in Quay, 185.
[7]Q. Scherman, quoted in Quay, 189.
[8]Quoted in Quay, 189.

cation for therapeutic abortion in the nineteen-twenties. For the most part, however, it has gone the same way as tuberculosis. As early as 1928 one source was able to point out that cardiologists had shown "that the heart can be treated successfully even though the woman is carrying the added burden of pregnancy."[9] A report on 568 pregnant women with rheumatic heart disease—none of whom had a therapeutic abortion—concluded: "It is probable that practically every pregnancy encountered in a patient with heart disease can be brought to a successful spontaneous termination if adequate prenatal care is instituted and if absolute bed rest is enforced when indicated."[10] Medical writers have also pointed to the fact that in any case heart patients "may be as poor surgical risks for abortion as they are obstetric risks."[11]

Dr. Guttmacher, writing in 1954, observed that "fewer and fewer patients are being aborted for cardiac disease." He went on to add:

Careful medical supervision with intelligent use of a salt-poor diet, weight control, diuretics, digitalis, antibiotics, anticoagulants, rest and improved anesthesia for delivery have made it possible for many cardiacs to have children who yesteryear would have been aborted, or who, unaborted, would perhaps have died. The care the patient takes of herself, and the

[9] Alfred C. Beck and Alexander H. Rosenthal, *Obstetrical Practice*, 7th ed. (Baltimore, 1958). Quoted in Quay, 190.
[10] H. Gorenberg, quoted in Quay, 191.
[11] Richard Te Linde, *Operative Gynecology* (Philadelphia, 1946). Quoted in Quay, 192.

quality of the medical care she receives, are almost as important as the gravity of the organic lesion. Even if the organic lesion is severe, the patient's desires should be given great weight, for no physician is astute enough to guarantee the performance of any serious cardiac in pregnancy, labor and puerperium. If the patient is extremely desirious of continuing the pregnancy, is able and willing to cooperate to the full, and knows the approximate risk involved, most obstetricians will allow pregnancy to continue. So far as we know, if the cardiac patient survives her accouchement, the disease is not rendered worse by the experience. On the other hand, if the severe cardiac patient cannot avail herself of proper care, or is resistant to undertaking the risk pregnancy implies, abortion is justified.[12]

Without dwelling on the matter here, it may be observed that the declaration of "justification" in the last sentence is based purely on predispositions, of the doctor, of the woman, and, presumably, of society at large. Those who oppose abortion would respond that "proper care" *should* be made available to all women, and all women *should* avail themselves of it. The statement as a whole, in any event, makes it apparent that there is no intrinsic reason why even serious heart disease should *demand* abortion.

Kidney disease. Chronic nephritis (Bright's Disease) has long been considered a strong indication for therapeutic abortion, "one of a diminishing few," it was remarked in 1932.[13] On the other hand, some authors have questioned whether pregnancy has any

[12]A. F. Guttmacher, quoted in Quay, 193.
[13]C. Cova, quoted in Quay, 191.

significant effect on the progress of this disease. Mortality rates for England and Wales from 1911 to 1922, for example, showed that more men than women died from chronic nephritis. Married and unmarried women up to the age of fifty-five showed the same mortality rate from this cause. It was argued, therefore, that treatment of the condition is more effective than abortion, besides having the additional advantage of avoiding the risk of hemorrhage or infection.[14] While a difference of opinion still seems to exist on the subject, it appears that there is a substantial body of opinion within the profession that sees nothing to be gained from abortion in such cases. "Here again," one writer observes, "more practical means of therapy have been devised" than abortion.[15]

Obviously it would be presumptuous for a layman, like the present author, to attempt to pass judgment in medical matters. These brief summaries of comments on certain so-called "indications" for therapeutic abortion do, however, show that specialists within the profession regard abortion in such cases as either unnecessary or of doubtful value. The same could be shown of many other "indications."[16]

Even so, opponents of abortion are prepared to admit that there may be conditions in which pregnancy constitutes a physical danger to the mother.

[14]R. J. Heffernan and W. A. Lynch, "Is Therapeutic Abortion Scientifically Justified?" *Linacre Quarterly* (1952).
[15]Q Scherman, quoted in Quay, 199.
[16]See Quay, 199-220.

"It would be wrong," one Catholic physician has written, "to give the impression that there are no circumstances in which the continuation of the pregnancy appears to offer a serious threat to the health or even to the life of the mother."[17] But it would be equally wrong to advance "indications" for abortion which are relatively trivial, or can be treated successfully by means short of destroying the life of the unborn child. As another physician has remarked:

> Pregnancy is a normal process. This has been taught for years. One wonders, then, why it is considered such a severe, and possibly fatal, burden when the pregnant woman develops a disease, or when a woman with a disease becomes pregnant. Or is the abortion which is recommended an indication of desperation, or a futile gesture of the physician to reach out blindly against a threat to his patient?[18]

DOES ABORTION DAMAGE HEALTH?

There is also another side to the coin: the evidence, by no means negligible, that induced abortion may damage the physical health of the mother. This is true not only of the operations performed by non-professional illegal abortionists, whose activities frequently result in "sterility, uterine deformation, (and) death,"[19] but also of those abortions performed

[17]John Marshall, M.D., *Medicine and Morals* (Glen Rock, N. J., 1964), p. 69.
[18]Cavanagh, 26.
[19]Dr. X, as told to Lucy Freeman, *The Abortionist* (New York, 1962), p. 20.

in hygienic conditions by qualified practitioners. Even here, it appears, undesirable physical after-effects can result.

The following account concerns abortion in Japan, the country which has one of the largest numbers of abortions annually of any nation in the world. Japan is in a position, if any country is, to show the consequences of widespread legalized abortion. Attributed to a public health nurse, the account covers other aftereffects of abortion besides physical ones, but these are probably inevitable, since there is apparently in some cases a relationship between psychic and physical states following abortion.

> Abortions are begun . . . at a young age, after (women) have given birth to . . . two children. The annual event becomes so tiresome that they choose sterilization when they reach about the age of thirty. About sixty per cent of these women . . . may be sterilized. During the early thirties complications also intensify; many complain of chronic headache and of dizziness; blood counts are low, faces sallow, blood pressure complications frequent. Women worry that the children might die, leaving them without support; they hope to give the best education to their two but are disappointed when they are not as bright as was hoped. Psychosomatic disturbances are on the increase; there are more tumors and cancerous growths. Older women are now inclined to oppose abortion and sterilization, having seen what is happening, but the younger ones feel confident and are caught in the tyranny of public opinion.[20]

[20]Anthony Zimmerman, S.V.D., *Catholic Viewpoint on Overpopulation* (Garden City, N. Y., 1961), pp. 90-91.

Other countries, too, have found abortion a questionable practice because of its effects upon the health of women. After abortion was legalized in Russia in 1920, the medical profession soon found that repeated abortions had a serious impact on a woman's health. Menstrual disturbances, endocrine problems, sterility and an increased incidence of ectopic pregnancies were noted.[21]

The Medical Association of Communist China in May, 1957, strongly opposed induced abortion for a variety of physiological and socioeconomic reasons. Among the grounds for opposition was the fact that induced abortion is "a hazardous operation and can subsequently lead to various physical discomforts and physiological irregularities."[22]

Advocates of easier abortion maintain, of course, that the operation is altogether safe—"safer than a tonsillectomy"[23]—and it would certainly be distorting facts to pretend that as a surgical procedure it is on a par for difficulty with, for example, brain surgery. At the same time, however, there is much testimony that abortion can have serious physical consequences, particularly when it is repeated. As one writer has said of abortion, "at best it subjects the woman to some immediate danger and ultimately

[21]Cavanagh, 57. Harriet F. Pilpel and Theodore Zavin, *Your Marriage and the Law* (New York, 1964), p. 196. Collier Books edition.

[22]Quoted in Cavanagh, 60.

[23]"The Scandal of Abortion—Laws," *The New York Times Magazine* (April 25, 1965).

to the risk of considerable physical deterioration."[24]
This is an aspect of the picture that the abortion
propagandists choose not to mention.

Gebhard and his colleagues report that among the
women they questioned, sixteen percent reported
unfavorable physical sequelae to abortion. These
included bleeding, cramps, temporary menstrual difficulties, or hospital stays of one or two days ("mildly
unfavorable"); more severe bleeding or cramping,
some infection, more than temporary menstrual difficulty, and hospital stays of several days ("mod-
erately unfavorable"); and septicemia, peritonitis,
other serious infections, long hospital stays, invalid-
ism, and near death ("severely unfavorable").[25]
Slightly more single women in their study reported
unfavorable results than did married women. Dr.
Hellegers suggests a sterility rate of two percent as
a not unreasonable estimate in abortions. Add to this
an approximate ten percent rate of moderate to
severe psychiatric consequences from abortion, he
says, "and you can perform your own mathematics
and arrive at the type of medical problem which
would appear on the American scene" in the event
of large-scale abortion in this country.[26]

[24]Fred J. Taussig, quoted in Quay, 224.
[25]Paul H. Gebhard, Wardell B. Pomeroy, Clyde E. Martin,
Cornelia V. Christenson, *Pregnancy, Birth and Abortion*
(New York, 1958), p. 206.
[26]Andre E. Hellegers, M.D., "A Doctor Looks at Abortion,"
in *Population Crisis*, hearings before the Subcommittee on
Foreign Aid Expenditures of the Committee on Government
Operations, United States Senate, Eighty-Ninth Congress,
Second Session, Part 5-B (Washington, 1967), p. 1391.

One may leave it to medical authorities to debate whether such figures make abortion a safe or an unsafe operation, as medicine understands "safety." What is evident, however, is that at least some degree of risk does accompany the artificial termination of pregnancy. Before the public at large—and healthy, pregnant women—are sold on the operation, honesty should oblige its proponents to publicize this fact. As one doctor has written:

> The operative hazards of a therapeutic abortion are as great as the hazards involved in the conservation of pregnancy in the best of institutions. According to Yoshio Koya, the eminent Japanese demographer, no less than 47% of women in Japan experience post-abortal complications. In Denmark, the incidence of serious, life-threatening complications is 3.2%. Such statistics suggest that the physical health of the mother will not be served by an increase in the number of therapeutic abortions.[27]

TECHNIQUES OF ABORTION

Most hospital abortions are carried out by the operation known as a "D and C"—dilatation and curettage. First the cervix is stretched by inserting a series of dilators of increasing size into the mouth of the womb. When the cervix is sufficiently dilated, the surgeon inserts the curette, a rake-shaped instrument, and with it scrapes the walls of the uterus and removes the embryo. In cases where abortion occurs

[27]Eugene F. Diamond, M.D., "The Doctor's Case Against Freer Abortion Laws," *Report*, February 1967.

after more than three months of pregnancy, a hysterotomy, involving an incision in the lower abdomen, is performed.

A more recent technique which may replace the hysterotomy involves the withdrawal by needle of some of the amniotic fluid which surrounds the fetus. It is replaced with a concentrated salt or glucose solution. The result is to induce labor, leading to the expulsion of the unborn child.

Another new method, limited to the first three months of pregnancy, has been developed in the Soviet Union. A tube is inserted into the uterus and suction applied, pulling loose the fetus and drawing it into the tube. One account of this technique adds laconically: "Tiny blades spin inside the tube, driven by a flexible rod in the tube. They facilitate removal of the material. . . ."[28]

Not yet available in this country but already attracting considerable attention are abortion "pills." A drug known as F-6103 has been tested for this purpose in Sweden. It is said to be effective as much as two months after conception. It is believed to work by interrupting the normal hormonal cycle of early pregnancy, thus causing the shedding of the lining of the uterus and the expulsion of the embryo. The drug's strong points are said to include not merely efficiency but psychological comfort as well. ". . . [N]o woman would even have to know whether

[28]*The New York Times,* June 4, 1967.

she was pregnant. She would not do any soul-searching. She would automatically take the pill once a month. Not ever having an unwanted pregnancy [that is, not one she knew about], she would never have to undergo surgery."[29] The same highly enthusiastic account notes that the developers of the new drug "prefer to call it the menstruation or M-pill, but much of the Swedish press refers to it as the A-pill, A for abortion."

Other synthetic compounds which operate like the female hormone estrogen are also under development. These drugs are designed to be taken post-coitally and act by preventing the implantation of the fertilized egg in the uterus.

Are such drugs, so-called "morning-after pills," true abortifacients? It appears that they are. Garrett Hardin, Professor of Biology at the University of California, Santa Barbara, says that a "retrospective" pill would operate either by preventing the implantation of "the barely started embryo" or causing it to be "sloughed off" soon after implantation; "it would be jesuitical of medical researchers to argue that either of these actions is not a true abortion."[30] Dr. Hardin, it should be noted, is one of those who looks forward to the perfecting of such drugs and to their unrestricted availability to all comers. "It is

[29]Ruth Link, "Those New Swedish Abortion Pills," *Ladies' Home Journal,* June 1967.
[30]Garrett Hardin, "The History and Future of Birth Control," *Perspectives in Biology and Medicine,* Vol. 10, No. 1 (Autumn 1966).

difficult to see," he writes, "that society has any interest in controlling the distribution of harmless abortifacients when they become available. Indeed, society has an interest in making them readily available to all, for only by giving women complete and sure control of births can we bring to a successful conclusion the emancipation of women begun more than a century ago."[31]

Accounts of abortion written by proponents generally go out of their way to minimize both the physical risk and the unpleasantness of the procedure. Occasionally, however, one does glimpse a different side to the story, as when one finds a prominent obstetrician remarking of abortion by dilatation and curettage that it "is the only operation done on an invisible field, with hemorrhage difficult to control."[32] Paul Ferris, a professed advocate of easier abortion, nevertheless concedes the repulsion that many members of the medical profession feel toward the operation. He explains:

> It is the only case in medicine, apart from cosmetic plastic surgery, where a healthy patient comes asking to have an operation. Add to this the objection that . . . the staff of the operating theatre may, if the pregnancy is advanced, see a miniature baby being removed and thrown away, and it is not hard to see why the average orthodox surgeon still tries to avoid it, and why, having done it, he compromises by writ-

[31]*Ibid.*
[32]Dr. Robert L. Dickinson, quoted in Gebhard et al., 193 (footnote).

ing "diagnostic D and C" when he is annotating the operation.[33]

Ferris also quotes a gynecologist as remarking of abortion: "I think it's one of the most revolting operations in the world. It's frightening because sometimes these patients bleed like stink, and also it's not difficult to perforate the uterus."[34]

The techniques of self-induced and illegal abortion are far more exotic than those of hospital abortion. In addition to surgical or quasi-surgical procedures, they include such things as the insertion of various objects and instruments into the uterus and drinking or eating such things as quinine, turpentine, ergot, aspirin, castor oil, Epsom salts, ammonia, beer, and water in which a rusty nail has been soaked. Dangerous as some of these procedures can be, and stringent as the legal punishment for them should be—particularly the punishment of those who perform illegal abortions for profit—it nevertheless appears that there is a good deal of exaggeration in popular accounts of illegal abortion. Gebhard and his colleagues found "a much higher quality of medical and surgical technique than much of the literature would lead one to expect" among the professional abortionists whom they interviewed.[35]

[33]Paul Ferris, *The Nameless: Abortion in Britain Today* (London, 1966), p. 139.
[34]Ferris, 167.
[35]Gebhard et al., 199.

THE FETUS

Neither medicine nor any other branch of science can settle whether the fetus is a human being. As Thomas L. Hayes, a biophysicist at the University of California, Berkeley, has remarked: "Science can only contribute in a secondary way to the solution of the question of the origin of the human individual. . . . [S]cience cannot lead theology, and for the theologian to limit such a definition of the human person to scientific qualities alone is to ignore the important personal and experienced modes of knowing reality."[36] Science can, however, provide some important indicators about the nature of the life developing within the womb of a pregnant woman. And what it tells must surely give any investigator pause as he contemplates the current rush to make it easier to destroy this life.

Thus, science tells us that at the moment of conception "an entirely new genetic package is created, unlike any other genetic package previously existent."[37] Immediately after the fusion of the male sperm and the female ovum the chromosomes of the new being line up to produce "a master plan for growth"[38] which will guide and condition the development of this

[36]Thomas L. Hayes, "A Biological View," *Commonweal*, March 17, 1967.

[37]Andre E. Hellegers, M.D., letter to the editor, *The National Catholic Reporter*, March 1, 1967.

[38]James C. G. Conniff, "The World of the Unborn," *The New York Times Magazine*, January 8, 1968.

new being throughout the rest of its life. Within five or six days of conception the embryo will have grown to 150 or more cells and will implant itself in the wall of the uterus. From this point on the formation of organs follows swiftly. By eight weeks the fetus will be "recognizably human,"[39] it will have limbs, its heart will have been beating for a week or more, its brain will emit and receive neurohormonal signals, and it will be identifiable as to sex. By the third month it will be about the size of an adult's thumb. It will be drinking some of the surrounding amniotic fluids, sucking and swallowing.

At what single point does the fetus acquire the biological form and function of a human person? Biology cannot say. Thomas Hayes writes:

> In fact, it appears that such a point does not exist. The attributes of form and function that designate the living system as a human individual are acquired at various times during development in a process that is relatively continuous. . . . The transition occurs gradually, not at a single point in time.[40]

It is worth noting, too, that the process of biological development by no means ends at birth. "The infant develops into the child, the child into the adult and even the adult continues to modify his form and function into old age and death."[41] Biologically, then, it is altogether arbitrary to say that the child before birth is not a human person and

[39]*Ibid.*
[40]Hayes, "A Biological View."
[41]*Ibid.*

may be killed, whereas the child after birth is a human person and may not be killed. The development of the human person is continuous throughout life, and anyone who argues in favor of the destruction of the child before birth can only be acting on a scientifically unverifiable presumption that he is not a human person. On the contrary, the "sound medical principle," as Dr. Andre Hellegers has said, is to give the benefit of the doubt to the presence of human life.

> We do not send patients to autopsy rooms if there is the slightest doubt that they might still be alive. . . . To give no benefit of the doubt to the fetus and argue when it becomes human is to return scientifically to debates about how many angels can dance on the head of a pin.
>
> We give blood transfusions to fetuses in utero at stages of development preceding those at which abortion is considered legal under some laws. The National Institute of Child Health and Development was set up to study the stages of human development from conception onwards. Learned journals speak about meetings of societies for the study of intra-uterine surgery. Popular newspapers talk about the development of a specialty called "fetology." In short, the scientific aspect of obstetrics has moved in a direction of accepting medical responsibility for the fetus in utero. It would be tragic if the medical profession, and especially the specialty of obstetrics and gynecology, were to become no more than the abortion technicians for the alleged solution of socio-economic problems which have no bearing on the primary specialty of medicine.[42]

[42]Hellegers, *National Catholic Reporter*.

The painful problem of fetal deformity, whether caused by rubella or other causes, has been discussed earlier.[43] It was noted that the evidence of prenatal deformity is at this point only statistical, and that statistical probabilities or possibilities should not be made to justify the taking of innocent life, particularly when, as in the case of rubella, six normal children may be destroyed for every four deformed ones. It was also noted that many of the defects produced by rubella and other causes are minor and correctible. It was noted finally that a civilized society simply does not kill its weaker members because of physical or mental handicaps, whether mild or severe. In this section on abortion and medicine, then, it need only be added that abortion in cases of suspected fetal abnormality really has nothing to do with medicine at all, but is rather performed for the psychological relief or the social, financial or aesthetic convenience of the child's parents.

Some of course may deny that this is so, but there is really no other tenable explanation. The argument that this is the only humane course of action with respect to the unborn child cannot be respected, for who knows what the unborn child's wishes in the matter are? There is simply no evidence that the crippled and the blind, for instance, would have preferred not to have lived than to have lived. Why then make this presumption in the case of an

[43]See above, pp. 14-20.

unborn child who cannot possibly speak for himself? The reason is that the "humane" argument is a mask for the desire of parents and society to spare themselves the expense, trouble and embarrassment that the deformed or otherwise abnormal child represents.

It is perfectly true that there are cases, even many cases, where an individual family is economically or emotionally unable to bear the burden of an abnormal child. Where this is so, however, the "humane" response is not killing the child but making provision to relieve the family of the burden it cannot support alone. "The only legitimate relief in such cases," says Rabbi Immanuel Jakobovits, "is for society to assume the burdens which the individual family can no longer bear. Since society is the main beneficiary of restrictive public laws on abortion (or homicide), it must in turn also pay the price sometimes exacted by these laws in the isolated cases demanding such a price."[44] What this means is the provision at public expense of financial support, services and, where necessary, institutional care for handicapped childern whose parents require such assistance.

THE "DISCRIMINATION" ARGUMENT

One of the arguments for easier abortion put forward in the medical context is the contention that present abortion laws in fact result in discrimination against

[44]Rabbi Dr. Immanuel Jakobovits, "Jewish Views on Abortion," in David T. Smith, ed., *Abortion and the Law* (Cleveland, 1967), p. 139.

the poor and the disadvantaged. It is pointed out that only seven percent of the hospital abortions in New York City in 1960-1962 were performed on non-whites, and that only eighty-two abortions in this time were performed on ward patients as against 792 on private patients.[45] Thus, liberalization of the law is said to be necessary to right the imbalance, and to make the blessing of abortion available to the non-white poor woman as well as the white affluent one.

The argument, however, does not stand up under close scrutiny. For one thing, ward patients as a rule register for prenatal care later in their pregnancies than do private patients.[46] What this means is that doctors generally see ward patients at a point in their pregnancies when abortion by dilatation and curettage is no longer possible, and the alternative is the risky method of abdominal surgery. The alleged "discrimination," in short, is simply a matter of sound medical procedure. Furthermore, as Lawrence Lader observes, the higher incidence of hospital abortion among the private patients simply reflects the success of "wealthy, influential women who can afford private rooms, and who can enlist the aid of specialists" in getting what they want.[47] It seems rather extraordinary to suggest that because people who

[45]Lawrence Lader, *Abortion* (New York, 1966), p. 29.
[46]Robert E. Hall, M.D., "Therapeutic Abortion, Sterilization, and Contraception," *American Journal of Obstetrics and Gynecology*, Vol. 91, No. 4 (February 15, 1965).
[47]Lader, 30.

are "wealthy" and "influential" can succeed in abus-
ing the laws, the same privilege of abuse should be
extended to those who are not wealthy and not
influential, or, more to the point, that the law should
be abrogated entirely so that everyone may be equal.
This is a strange principle on which to base one's
approach to the law. As one writer has remarked,
the argument that the law must be changed because
"the wealthy can get an abortion more easily than
the poor" is "somewhat like saying that if a man
is wealthy enough to move to a Moslem country and
marry four wives, we must change the bigamy laws
here because the poor are being discriminated
against."[48]

It is also said that laws against abortion are an
infringement on the rights of doctors, who must have
absolute autonomy to treat their patients as they see
fit. Other medical procedures are not subjected to
such stringent legal control, so there is no reason
why abortion should be.

To one who is not a physician, this argument has
a strange sound. In any reasonable view of the matter, abortion is a life-and-death matter with implications that go far beyond the autonomy of the medical profession. No one wants to see doctors over
controlled, but neither does one want them to be
under controlled, and it would seem that in the ques-

---

[48]Andre E. Hellegers, M.D., "Law and the Common
Good," *Commonweal*, June 30, 1967.

tion of abortion the interests of society transcend those of the medical profession's right to regulate itself. This view of the matter is shared by segments of the profession itself. A writer in the *Canadian Medical Association Journal* notes, for instance, the danger that "a medical morality may come to be substituted for a much wider human morality, and it is this substitution that is suggested by the proposal that the question of abortion be settled solely on medical grounds."[49]

Some doctors, of course, feel no hesitation about ignoring the laws on abortion. These include men like Dr. G. Loutrell Timanus of Baltimore, lionized by the pro-abortion movement, who operated as an abortionist for twenty-five years before being convicted in 1951 and sentenced to a jail term and a $5,000 fine, and who now describes himself as "an incorrigible crusader against the hypocrisy and inhumanity of our system";[50] or Lawrence Lader's "Dr. S.," said to have performed more than 28,000 abortions, whose motto is "Electricity and God are One."[51]

While some physicians may feel a certain moralistic zeal in performing abortions, others exhibit less desirable motives. Power is one; money is another. Says Dr. Herbert Ratner, Director of Public Health in Oak Park, Illinois: "The liberty to abort makes the

[49]C. P. Harrison, "On the Futility of Legalizing Abortion," *The Canadian Medical Association Journal,* August 20, 1966.
[50]Quoted in Lader, 43.
[51]Lader, 45.

physician more like a god than is good for him. Abortions are also lucrative. We've experienced the prevalence of unnecessary operations. We must face it: anything that comes along that is a money maker is most seductive to the medical profession especially when combined with godliness. After all we physicians are only human beings and we are immersed in a materialistic society."[52]

There is a danger here for both doctors and the public, a danger that transcends the limited issue of abortion. It is that, operating under the rubric of "science," physicians may claim, and the public grant them, competence in areas beyond their special sphere of knowledge and skill. Warning of the dangers of "medical paternalism," Father Gerald Vann, O.P., a prominent British moralist, writes:

Science, we know, is concerned with facts and with the patterns-of-facts which we call physical laws: it can give us knowledge about these facts, it has no competence whatsoever to tell us how, or if, to use our knowledge. It can tell us how to do things; it cannot possibly tell us whether or not we ought to do them. But the long reign of assumed omnicompetence lingers on, like its materialist postulates, in a sort of unconscious atmosphere which is difficult to dispel; and here therefore it is science which must be blamed, and blamed not merely for going beyond its sphere of competence, but for being unscientific—for it is unscientific for science to claim omnicompetence and therefore autonomy.[53]

[52]"A Doctor Talks About Abortion," *Report,* April, 1966.
[53]Gerald Vann, O.P., *Moral Dilemmas* (Garden City, N.Y., 1965), pp. 48-49.

Theology, Father Vann adds, has no right to tell medicine how to cure a disease or to interfere in scientific studies as such. But at the same time "of its nature it must be concerned to regulate them extrinsically *ex alto* by subsuming them under the ultimate principles which govern man's pursuit of his destiny."[54]

In many cases whether or not an abortion is performed is determined by the prior attitudes of patients and doctors rather than by the therapeutic requirements of the situation. This is evident from, among other sources, the striking record of the Margaret Hague Maternity Hospital in Jersey City, New Jersey, whose experience was related by Dr. Joseph P. Donnelly, its medical director, at the previously mentioned symposium sponsored by the Planned Parenthood Federation.[55]

Dr. Donnelly reported that the Hague Hospital had performed a total of eight therapeutic abortions in more than 150,000 deliveries. Responding to the unspoken question, "How did the Margaret Hague Hospital get that way?" he went on to explain:

> First of all, the Margaret Hague Hospital is not a Catholic hospital. Doctor Cosgrove, who was the first medical director and who has been there for some years, is not a Catholic. The majority of the attending staff are not Catholics. However, Hudson County is a

[54]Vann, 51-52.
[55]See Calderone, 102-103.

Catholic community with a population about seventy-five percent Catholic, largely educated in parochial schools, and well aware of the church's teaching in regard to abortion.

The influence of this population has had a definite effect on the Margaret Hague Hospital. In the early days of the hospital, which opened in 1931, we had many long staff conferences concerning therapeutic abortions. Doctor Cosgrove and other members of the staff thought at the time that therapeutic abortions should occasionally be done for medical indications. However, a good number of patients refused a recommended therapeutic abortion so that we had to take care of them through their pregnancy, and we were very much surprised that they didn't do as badly as everybody else said they would. There was no doubt that the attitude of the patients had a definite effect on the attitude of the staff concerning this matter.

Dr. Donnelly went on to cite the Hague Hospital's record of eight abortions in 150,000 deliveries. By contrast, he noted, if the hospital had performed abortions in just one percent of all deliveries, or ten per thousand—"not a high figure when compared with other clinics"—1,500 pregnancies would thus have been aborted. "Even with one-third spontaneous fetal mortality among those fifteen hundred we did *not* abort, this still leaves a thousand children alive today who would not be alive if our incidence of therapeutic abortion had been one percent," he remarked.

The doctor cautioned his colleagues against allowing themselves to be influenced too heavily by nonmedical considerations in making up their minds about abortion. "We should be doctors of medicine, not socio-economic prophets," he commented, adding:

Slums and delinquency exist. It may seem very easy to sit around here and say that certain cases will be aborted and that will solve the problem, but I am afraid it is going to take public housing, good health care, high minimum wages, family allowances, and the general raising of the standards of the American people to solve these problems. It looks very easy to eliminate the unfit and the poor socio-economic risks from our civilization with the curette and thereby to build a better society, but I think it is simply a distinction without a difference between this type of reasoning and the reasoning of a man of unhappy memory who thought he could raise the standards of society by eliminating the so-called unfit with the gas chambers of Buchenwald.

IV

Abortion and Psychiatry

Psychiatric indications, so-called, probably account for more legal abortions at present than any other cause. This, however, does not mean that psychiatric indications for abortion have been increasing in recent years. It is rather a reflection of the fact that as the total number of legal, hospital abortions has declined, due to the drop-off in the number of abortions performed for physiological reasons, abortions performed on nominally psychiatric grounds have accounted for a larger proportion of the falling total.[1] Nevertheless, the incidence of psychiatric abortion has declined in recent years, too. Thus, whereas prior to 1950 one pregnancy in every 1,021 was terminated by abortion on psychiatric grounds at Johns Hopkins Hospital, since 1950 the incidence has been only one in 2,231.[2] A psychiatrist, reviewing advances in therapy, concludes that "before too long, most psychiatrists, in most cases, may have virtually no valid grounds for approving abortion."[3]

[1]Andre E. Hellegers, M.D., "Law and the Common Good," *Commonweal*, June 30, 1967.
[2]*Ibid.*
[3]Frank J. Ayd, M.D., "Liberal Abortion Laws: A Psychiatrist's View," in *The Reasons Against Abortion*, a col-

Still, the popular mythology of abortion gives heavy emphasis to psychiatric indications for termination of pregnancy. The distraught, suicidal woman trapped by a calamitous pregnancy is a stock figure of the scenarios promulgated for popular consumption by the abortion law reformers. In view of this emphasis, then, it is curiously difficult to find a clear explanation of the psychiatric indications for abortion. There seem to have been few attempts to spell out whether the notion refers to the likelihood of a complete mental and emotional breakdown of the mother during pregnancy, of such dimensions as to make institutionalization necessary, or whether on the contrary the concept of psychiatric indications includes only a limited degree of emotional stress and strain. If the latter is the case, one might wonder whether any pregnancy is ever free of such indications.

It is not even clear whether the indications encompass problems that will occur before the birth of the child or after. One finds authors speaking of the emotional burden to be borne by mothers of several children who soon will have to care for yet another. In such cases, however, the psychiatric indications are of course purely speculative—clouds on the horizon rather than a present storm—based on the assumption that the mother will experience emo-

lection of testimony before the Codes and Health Committees of the New York Legislature, February 3, 8 and 10, 1967, distributed by the New York State Catholic Welfare Committee (mimeographed).

tional distress in attempting to care for the new child. It seems obvious also that in such cases a psychiatrist's preexisting attitudes toward abortion will play a large part in his decision on whether or not to recommend termination of pregnancy. As Dr. Frank Ayd has said, "It depends as much on the personal conviction of the psychiatrist and the prevailing social climate as on established psychiatric facts."[4]

In cases where emotional difficulty is anticipated rather than already present, the problem, rather than being directly produced by the pregnancy, will on the contrary only become a reality after the child has been born. Termination of pregnancy in such circumstances does not solve an existing problem but only seeks to forestall a problem which not even the psychiatrist can be certain will ever exist. Psychiatrists are far from infallible in such matters. Dr. Myre Sim, Consultant Psychiatrist, United Birmingham Hospitals (England), has recalled his own experience in the case of a schizophrenic woman who had been in a mental hospital for eighteen months and subsequently became pregnant after being released in the care of her husband. Dr. Sim described her case as a "classical indication" and recommended abortion.

> However, this patient showed some volition and said that she didn't want to have her baby taken away. We were surprised; we even thought that this was evidence of her mental illness. The only way that we

[4]*Ibid.*

could terminate her to protect her mental health would have been to certify her and do it against her will— a very unpleasant thing to think of, far less to do. And so I said, "Well, she is pretty bad, she can't be made much worse by her pregnancy, let's take the line of least resistance and let her go on." She went to term, had the baby and, to our surprise, got better. We watched her to see if she would relapse but she continued well.[5]

For one who is not already committed to abortion or who takes the destruction of innocent life seriously, the question must inevitably arise whether abortion is an appropriate measure for dealing with the difficulties of a woman who has, or is on the verge of having, more children than she can cope with. In many distress cases assistance in homemaking and child care would be more to the point—would be a more genuine service—than abortion. But such solutions involve compassion and expense. The curette provides an apparently neater and simpler answer— an answer which perhaps seems irresistible to one who does not attach much importance to the life of the fetus; hence the "psychiatric" abortion.

Even in cases of genuine, existing emotional problems, there are solutions besides abortion, at least for those who wish to use them. So far as actual psychiatric therapy is concerned, Dr. John Marshall has pointed to the "extremely relevant fact" that other

[5]Myre Sim, M.D., "Psychiatric Indications for Abortion," address to the British Medical Advisers Conference, May, 1966.

methods of treatment are often available but are not used.

> A non-pregnant woman who is depressed may be treated by drugs, electro-convulsive therapy or by a period in hospital, and make a good recovery. Why should not a pregnant woman be similarly treated? Why, in this instance, should the life of a child be sacrificed, rather than the treatment applied which would be used in the non-pregnant state?[6]

As with therapeutic abortion, there is another side to the coin of psychiatric abortion, the question of whether termination of pregnancy does the woman more harm than good. At the very least it appears that the results of the operation may go either way, and that it is difficult to predict whether the outcome will be good or bad in the long run. A physician participating in the Planned Parenthood symposium mentioned above remarked that he sometimes wished he were an obstetrician in a Catholic hospital "so that I would not have to make any of these decisions."[7] He explained: "The only position to take in which I would have no misgivings is to do no interruption of pregnancy at all. All so-called indications have a relative value only." But if that is the case, or if a physician feels that way, it is pertinent to ask why he should recommend any abortions at all. One explanation, as we shall see below, is that physicians

[6]John Marshall, M.D., *Medicine and Morals* (Glen Rock, N.J., 1964), p. 69.
[7]Mary Steichen Calderone, M.D., ed., *Abortion in the United States* (New York, 1958), p. 123.

and psychiatrists are subject to, and sometimes succumb to, pressures to conform, socially and professionally, or to oblige influential or insistent patients.

The pressures operate in both directions of course, sometimes from the patient to the doctor, and sometimes from the doctor to the patient. Dr. Harold Rosen, a psychiatrist who favors abortion for any woman who wants it—"Mature women, as mature human beings with all the respect and dignity to be accorded mature human beings, should have the right to decide whether or not they wish to carry a specific pregnancy to term"[8]—has also explained how pressures from a physician may force a woman into seeking, on psychiatric grounds, an abortion she does not really want.

> A woman who says she wants an abortion sometimes comes to the psychiatrist not because she wants it but because she has come to sense that her obstetrician or her family physician or the uncle-physician who would never consciously think of suggesting an abortion to her, nevertheless feels it a pity for her to be pregnant and somehow, without saying so, gets her to realize that he wants her to interrupt it. I have seen this on numerous occasions. Give that woman a chance to talk after she comes to the psychiatrist and asks for an abortion, and she herself will tell you this and talk herself out of wanting it! Of course, the psychiatrist can never let the obstetrician or the physician involved know all that, but it does happen.[9]

[8]Harold Rosen, M.D. "Psychiatric Implications of Abortion: A Case Study in Social Hypocrisy," in David T. Smith, ed., *Abortion and the Law* (Cleveland, 1967), p. 106.
[9]Calderone, 124.

(In passing, it is of some interest that the above comment by Dr. Rosen appears in a book published in 1958, while his assertion of the right of any woman to have an abortion if she wants it appears in a book published in 1967. It would be even more interesting to know how Dr. Rosen reconciles his argument for the unrestricted right of women to be aborted if they choose with his earlier admission that some women who "choose" abortion are actually being pressured into it—"I have seen this on numerous occasions." One doubts that the sort of pressures described by Dr. Rosen in 1958 had magically vanished by 1967.)

But if doctors can pressure patients into having abortions, patients can also pressure doctors and psychiatrists. In a British provincial hospital, Dr. Sim remarks, it is easy enough for psychiatrists to turn down requests for abortion, but it is considerably harder in a metropolitan center like London. "If you're dealing with V.I.P.s, Stock Exchange families, the daughter of an ambassador, the pressure to abort must be greater."[10] Paul Ferris asserts that some psychiatrists in recommending abortions "let themselves be used as a social convenience because of the money."[11] Ferris reports his interview with a London psychiatrist who spoke of "at least a dozen" colleagues who "always said Yes."

[10]Quoted in Paul Ferris, *The Nameless: Abortion in Britain Today* (London, 1966), p. 131.
[11]Ferris, 132.

"It makes the name of psychiatry stink," he said, and added that a neighbor of his would "see twelve patients in a morning for termination of pregnancy and never say No." Gynaecologists used him, he said, not only for his tractability but because "they know he can write well. His opinion would be clinically unassailable in the courts. It wouldn't be unassailable at the Royal Society of Medicine—they'd laugh at him there—but it has sufficient clinical criteria to assuage the anxiety of the surgeon. It provides cover for the job." If I required a piece of foolproof evidence, he suggested I hire a young actress and send her with a hard-luck pregnancy story to an easy psychiatrist, who would listen to a pack of lies and certify that she needed an abortion; he added that she wouldn't have to be a very good actress.[12]

HOW NECESSARY IS ABORTION?

How necessary is abortion on psychiatric grounds? Dr. Rosen states that most indications for abortion are "mere rationalizations." "The medical, including the psychiatric, indications must be utilized if the abortion is to have legal justification. However, in most cases, the socioeconomic factors are pronounced; and whether the interruption of the pregnancy is legal or extralegal, the actual indications are, for the most part, socioeconomic."[13]

One situation which would seem to offer a compelling argument for terminating pregnancy arises when a pregnant woman in a depressed state threatens to commit suicide if she is obliged to go on

[12]Ferris, 133.
[13]Rosen in Smith, 87.

carrying her child. It is easy to see how all involved might regard abortion as the best step in such a case. A closer analysis, however, suggests otherwise.

There is, to begin with, a question as to just how seriously one should take such a suicide threat. Dr. Howard C. Taylor, Jr., Director of Obstetrical and Gynecological Service, Columbia-Presbyterian Medical Center, New York, commenting on the "subterfuges" employed to obtain abortions on psychiatric grounds, described himself as "very much disturbed by the use of the indication of reactive depression with suicidal tendency" as an argument for abortion. "I have not in my experience ever run across a suicide in pregnancy in a patient who was suffering from anxiety depression," he stated.[14] The same point has been made by Dr. Theodore Lidz, Professor of Psychiatry at the Yale University School of Medicine. He said:

> Let us be frank about this. When the psychiatrist says that there is a suicidal risk, in many instances he does not mean that at all, but feels there are strong socio-economic grounds for a therapeutic abortion. Since the only ground for abortion in many states is if it is felt there is threat of death, suicidal risk is thus established as the only legal way out of the situation.[15]

Some, of course, will see in such a remark an argument for making it easier to get abortions on socioeconomic grounds. (One is reminded of Kenneth

[14]Calderone, 108.
[15]Calderone, 141.

R. Niswander and Morton Klein's sympathetic view of the forty-year-old divorced woman who is carrying an illegitimate child and wants an abortion—on "psychogenic" grounds—in order to "maintain her social status."[16]) Others, however, will only find in it reason for taking talk about indications for abortion with a grain or more of salt. It is also worth recalling that, as psychiatrists are well aware, patients are quite capable of developing—sincerely and in good faith—the symptoms that the situation seems to call for. As one physician has remarked of abortion, "the situation is one of the few in medicine where the patient may have an interest in deceiving the doctor."[17] If, then, suicidal depression were to be accepted as grounds for abortion, it might be expected that some women who either consciously or unconsciously wished their pregnancies terminated would exhibit symptoms of this condition, simply as a means of obtaining the desired abortion. It might also be expected that doctors who wished to abort would go out of their way to find the necessary grounds. As Paul Ferris says, "emotional instability is what the interrogator is looking for and what he manages to find. The more lax doctors ask leading questions."[18] A married woman who underwent an abortion has reported:

[16]Kenneth R. Niswander and Morton Klein, quoted in Lawrence Lader, *Abortion* (New York, 1966), p. 150.

[17]Quoted in Ayd, "Liberal Abortion Laws: A Psychiatrist's View."

[18]Ferris, 114

You have to make out that you're not mentally fit to have a baby if you don't want it, because although they are prepared to do it in the end, you know, they just don't give in immediately. I think they're rather sadistic. . . . You have to cry and get hysterical about it, and they write it all down—"She got hysterical in my office, and I'm sure she'll kill herself."[19]

All this, of course, would be somewhat beside the point if there were evidence that pregnant women are considerable suicide risks. But the evidence points in just the other direction. Says Dr. Rosen: "It should be noted . . . that although one successful suicide does occur every half hour in this country, the suicide rate among pregnant women is less than what would statistically be expected for the population as a whole. The Chief Medical Examiner of the State of Maryland, for instance, could 'recall only one pregnancy among the last 700 suicides. . . .' "[20] Dr. Sim reports that over a six-year period 120 women of child-bearing age committed suicide in the city of Birmingham, England; not one was pregnant. Over a second six-year period, one pregnant woman committed suicide, and in her case "abortion was not the answer, and it would not have cured her mental illness." Noting that "it has been held that pregnancy is almost a prophylactic against suicide," Dr. Sim concludes: "The best advice a doctor can give a pregnant woman who threatens suicide is tell her to stay pregnant."[21]

[19]Quoted in Ferris, 114.
[20]Rosen in Smith, 83.
[21]Sim, "Psychiatric Indications for Abortion."

Obviously not all doctors feel that way. Ferris reports the case of a London psychiatrist who recommended abortion for an unmarried, nineteen-year-old girl on the grounds that she was "anxious, acutely depressed and near breaking down." During questioning later by the police, "someone put it to the psychiatrist that there was nothing unusual about an unmarried girl being upset to find she was pregnant; but the psychiatrist kept repeating that his decision was based on long experience."[22] Ferris also notes that "many psychiatrists do have a financial interest in recommending an abortion"; and while individual doctors certainly may recommend termination of pregnancy in good faith, "it is . . . the chorus of suicide threats that sounds suspicious."[23] Whether or not the doctors are in good faith, it is clear enough that the patients are not always. Of suicidal threats as means of obtaining abortion, Doctors Leopold and Rudiger Breitenecker remark laconically: "The latter are frequently used to obtain permission for abortion by putting the psychiatrist under duress."[24] Dr. Sim speaks more colorfully of the "pseudocide": "Because the threat of suicide is regarded as an indication for abortion this tends to stimulate and foster such attempts. We would probably see much less of it if it were generally accepted that suicide risk is not

[22]Ferris, 126.
[23]Ferris, 130-31.
[24]Leopold Breitenecker, M.D., and Rudiger Breitenecker, M.D., "Abortion in the German-Speaking Countries of Europe," in Smith, 222.

regarded as an indication for termination of pregnancy."[25]

There is evidence that, from the psychiatric point of view, the begetting and raising of children is not merely optional for married persons but is truly necessary for their personal fulfilment and indeed for their mental health. "This acceptance of a child," one author says, "is in accord with nature and any persistent frustration of this natural longing may be expected to have deleterious effects of a psychological nature."[26]

> There is at any time an intensified feeling of guilt over the destruction of new life even in the case of many innocent women who suffer strong feelings of guilt as the result of spontaneous abortions or miscarriages which they have not willed directly. . . . In those cases where there is a conscious wish, any small accident may be considered by the woman as intended and, if followed by a termination of her pregnancy, she may consider it as deliberately induced. This may then be followed by strong feelings of guilt. If such guilt arises in an involuntary spontaneous abortion it would indeed be intensified in an abortion which was voluntarily sought.[27]

Abortions do not occur in a psychological vacuum. They are preceded by and are to some extent the result of preexisting psychological states: conditions which themselves need and deserve better treatment

[25]Sim, "Psychiatric Indications for Abortion."
[26]John R. Cavanagh, M.D., manuscript entitled *Abortion: Another Look,* p. 42.
[27]Cavanagh, 39.

than the at best expedient, and at worst harmful, measure of terminating the pregnancy. According to Dr. Iago Galdston, Executive Secretary of the Medical Information Bureau, New York Academy of Medicine:

> If and when a so-called adult woman, a responsible female, seeks an abortion, unless the warrant for it is overwhelming—as say in the case of rape or incest —we are in effect confronted both with a sick person and sick situation. Furthermore, and I want strongly to underscore this point, neither the given person nor the given situation is likely to be remedied by the abortion, *qua* abortion. It is, of course, true that both the person and the situation may be relieved and somewhat ameliorated by the abortion, much as an individual suffering from a gangrenous foot may be relieved by an amputation of the affected member,[28] but I would like to go on record that in numerous instances both the individual and the situation are actually aggravated rather than remedied by the abortion. Bad as the situation was initially, it not infrequently becomes worse after the abortion has taken place.[29]

In view of this fact it is ironic that, as Dr. Ayd has remarked, "very few women considered for abortion on psychiatric grounds, whether aborted or not, actually have any psychiatric treatment."[30]

[28]This is an unfortunate analogy, to say the least. The child is not a part of the mother's body, like her foot or her hand, but is a human person with his own right to live. Nor is there, presumably, anything wrong with the child; the problem, in the case of psychiatric "indications," is on the mother's side, not his.

[29]Calderone, 119.

[30]Ayd, "Liberal Abortion Laws: A Psychiatrist's View."

HOW ABORTION CAN DO HARM

In what ways does or can the situation become, in
Dr. Galdston's word, "worse" as a result of abortion?
This has been explained in some detail by psychiatrists. Before going on to examine the mental
and emotional disorders that can arise from abortion,
however, it may be best first to survey the statistical
evidence of bad psychological consequences from
abortion.

A number of studies have been published on this
subject. It is probably true, as the authors of a recent
survey article remark, that there remains a "lack of
conclusive data" about the effects of abortion on
the mental health of women.[31] Nevertheless, the find-
ings presently available constitute a rather per-
suasive body of evidence pointing to the fact that
the psychiatric "sequelae" of abortion can be bad—
sometimes extremely so. Thus, for example, Ekblad
in a study of 479 Swedish women who underwent
abortion found that 14 percent experienced mild
reproach and regret, 11 percent serious reproach and
regret, and 1 percent serious post-abortion psychiatric illness.[32] Arens studied 248 women who had
legal abortions in Sweden. He found 23 percent
with severe guilt and 25 percent with mild guilt.

[31]Nathan M. Simon, M.D., and Audrey G. Senturia, "Psychiatric Sequelae of Abortion," *Archives of General Psychiatry*, Vol. 15 (October 1966).
[32]N. Ekblad, "Induced Abortion on Psychiatric Grounds,"
Acta Psychiat. Scand., suppl., p. 99, 1955.

Among the symptoms of those with severe guilt were insomnia, decreased work capacity and nervousness.[33] Malmfors reported on eighty-four women who had legal abortions in Sweden. Of this group, four indicated embarrassment and distress and did not like to talk about their experience; nine were classified as consciously repressing guilt feelings; twenty-two had open feelings of guilt; and ten were classified as having suffered impairment of their mental health.[34]

Depression and guilt feelings are the most frequently cited adverse psychological consequences of abortion. Dr. Rosen has noted that psychiatrists encounter patients who, after undergoing abortion, "accused themselves shortly afterwards or even after the passage of years, of being murderesses and then go into very pronounced depressive reactions."[35] Further, he notes, such patients sometimes seek punishment either for themselves or for the person they hold responsible for having forced abortion on them, most frequently their husbands. Thus: "We see patients who deliberately afterward punish themselves or their husbands by forcing vasectomy upon them, or in other ways—sometimes unconsciously, but very frequently on conscious levels deliberately castrating their husbands—usually

[33]P. Arens, in *Yearbook of Obstetrics and Gynecology* (Chicago, 1958-59), p. 64.
[34]K. Malmfors, in Calderone, 133-35.
[35]Calderone, 129.

emotionally, but occasionally even in actuality."[36]
Dr. Rosen observes, of course, that such adverse
consequences do not *have* to occur and indeed "frequently" do not. Still, the fact that they do appear
in a certain number of cases raises serious questions
about the appropriateness of abortion from a psychiatric point of view. It seems rather beside the
point to argue, as one physician did, that there is no
particular risk of guilt following abortion—because
he had observed patients who admitted to as many
as fifteen to twenty self-induced abortions without
exhibiting any signs of guilt or depression.[37] The
mildest comment to be made about such a group
of women is that they are atypical; the strongest
is that one wonders what, if anything, they *would*
feel guilty about. In any case one has the contrary
testimony of psychiatrist-members of the Group for
the Advancement of Psychiatry, who in their study,
Sex and the College Student, conclude that "for an
unmarried girl, the destruction of the fetus is an
overwhelming reality about which she may sooner
or later become deeply concerned."[38] It is also significant that these psychiatrists question the commonly held notion that legalizing abortion will remove a guilt-inducing circumstance from the
operation.

[36]*Ibid.*

[37]Arthur J. Mandy, M.D., "Reflections of a Gynecologist,"
in Harold Rosen, M.D., ed., *Abortion in America* (Boston,
1967), p. 292, paperback edition.

[38]Group for the Advancement of Psychiatry, *Sex and the
College Student* (New York, 1965), p. 52.

Much has been written about the possible emotional effects of the furtive and sordid atmosphere in which illegal abortions are performed; in practice, we observe that the traumatic results of a legal abortion are not necessarily less severe than those of a criminal one. We suspect, in fact, that there may be more unresolved conflict in feelings when the abortion is legal, simply because this type of abortion is usually arranged for the student by someone else (parent, family doctor), while the young woman herself usually takes the active responsibility in arranging for criminal abortion. As a result, legal or therapeutic abortions may be performed in many cases where the wish for them is ambivalent and where they might not have been performed at all without the active involvement of others. . . . Even the medically justified and well-intentioned recommendation for therapeutic abortion can have the unexpected result of confirming a girl's unconscious fears of being unworthy to bear a child.[39]

Dr. Theodore Lidz suggests that guilt feelings associated with abortion are not simply the product of religious and moral conditioning but arise from something deeper in human nature. Such feelings, he says, may have "far more vitally to do with the woman's feeling that she is destroying . . . something that is properly her goal in life." And, along with guilt, he notes, the woman experiences a "loss of self-esteem" at being willing to sacrifice her unborn child for the sake of some selfish interests of her own—her job, her relationship with her husband, or whatever it may be. Another aspect of this loss of self-esteem is bound up with the woman's chagrin

[39]*Ibid.*

if she is suffering mental illness in the first place—
an experience that heightens her feelings of in-
adequacy. To tell such a woman that because of her
mental condition she should undergo an abortion
"simply increases her feelings of worthlessness."[40]
A British psychiatrist notes that in some patients
termination of pregnancy may provoke guilt and
depression which are "less accessible to psycho-
therapy even than the pregnancy," although this
is "rare in practice." He describes it as "the considered opinion of many that if more psychiatric
sessions were available at ante-natal clinics, many
patients now recommended for termination could
safely be got through their pregnancy."[41] Women
who have undergone induced abortions, Dr. Lidz
remarks, often suffer from fear of punishment—not
only in the next life but in this one as well. "A
common form . . . is the feeling that because of the
abortion she may not be able to conceive again, or
will develop a malignancy." In reaction to such feelings, such a woman may turn to self-punishment
for her action: "perhaps an increased drive to
achievement in other fields, or a general masochistic
attitude toward the world."[42]

In such a situation it is not surprising that the

[40]Richard P. Vaughan, S. J., "Psychotherapeutic Abortion,"
America, October 16, 1965.

[41]*Abortion, An Ethical Discussion,* published for the
Church Assembly Board for Social Responsibility by the
Church Information Office (London, 1965), p. 64.

[42]See Calderone, 125-27.

woman's relationship with her husband should suffer
if he is the one who has compelled her to undergo
the abortion. V. C. Hamilton, who interviewed 100
women who had undergone abortions at Bellevue
Hospital and returned for checkups subsequent
to their release, found that fifteen of the seventy
women who had initially said they loved and respected their male partners now reported mixed
emotions or dislike; in thirteen cases the relationship
which led to the pregnancy had been terminated
and feelings of dislike and repugnance were reported; of sixty-eight women who initially reported
positive feelings toward sexual relations, ten now
disliked them and twenty-two were now indiffer-
ent.[43] Dr. Lidz says the woman will have "a
number of resentments toward him [the father];
his desire to have intercourse, to have what *he*
wants, while *she* must degrade herself to have an
abortion; the feeling that he should have made it
possible, somehow, for her to go on to have the baby;
the feelings that the man considers his career of
more importance to him than the baby is to her. . . ."
Even if the woman manages to persuade herself
rationally that the abortion was justified, "she will
harbor all these feelings to the point of not wanting
to have intercourse with him."[44]

[43]V. C. Hamilton, "Medical Status and Psychologic Attitudes of Patients Following Abortion," *American Journal of
Obstetrics and Gynecology*, Vol. 41, 285-287 (Jan.-June
1941).
[44]Calderone, 125-27.

Nor are these psychological consequences necessarily manifested at once or of brief duration. Bolter states that patients who have undergone an abortion may develop emotional disorders years later which reach a climax at menopause.[45] Particularly in involutional melancholia, Lidz says, "feelings aroused at the time of an abortion performed many years previously can become reactivated to be the focus of the self-derogation that depresses the aging patient."[46]

Others have issued similar warnings. Nicholson J. Eastman, for example, has called abortion on psychiatric grounds "a double-edged sword which may aggravate rather than ameliorate psychotic tendencies."[47] Gunard A. Nelson has warned that induced abortion "may cause great emotional trauma and may even induce psychosis in a patient with a poorly integrated personality."[48] This, of course, raises the question whether abortion is not likely to do the most psychological damage to the woman for whom presumptively it is most likely to be recommended, the woman, that is, who is already suffering from an emotional disorder. This is Dr. Sim's conclusion: "[T]he person who is at greatest risk is the very person whom you might consider for an

[45]S. Bolter, "The Psychiatrist's Role in Therapeutic Abortion: The Unwitting Accomplice," *American Journal of Psychiatry*, Vol. 119, 312-318 (1962).
[46]Calderone, 125-27.
[47]Quoted in Cavanagh, 49.
[48]*Ibid.*

abortion. This is the paradox in recommending termination. A slap-happy rather chancy girl, easy in her ways, probably won't come to you—she knows where to go in any case—because she doesn't need the blessing of the doctor. The girl who wants the blessing of the doctor wants sanction for her abortion and that in itself is a pointer that she is carrying a fair load of potential guilt. She is the very person whom you must be very careful not to abort because she is the one who is at risk from post abortive psychosis."[49]

An even darker side to the picture appears when one considers the problem of suicide and abortion. It was noted above that medical authorities seriously question whether there is any real danger that a pregnant woman will commit suicide for psychiatric reasons if she is denied an abortion. Indeed, the point was made that the suicide threat may be a sort of scare technique employed by women and their physicians to obtain sanction for otherwise illegal operations.

But the other side of this matter is whether abortion sometimes leads to suicide in women suffering guilt feelings as a result of having submitted to an induced termination of pregnancy. Though the evidence on this point is inconclusive, it is at least worth reflection that the two highest suicide rates in the world for women in the twenty to twenty-four age bracket are those of Japan (44.1 per

[49]Sim, "Psychiatric Indications for Abortion."

100,000) and Hungary (17.1 per 100,000)—two countries whose abortion rates are among the world's highest. This has led Professor Shiden Inoue of Japan's Nanzan University to suggest a possible "causal relationship" between abortion and suicide in these two countries.[50]

Finally, in discussing the psychiatric aspects of abortion, mention should be made of the problem of the "unwanted" child. Is it fair to require parents to shoulder the burden of a child whose conception may have been an undesired accident and whose birth and rearing they feel will be onerous and distasteful to them? And what of the child in these circumstances? Should he be forced to enter life with the handicap of having one or both parents resentful of his very existence? Developing these lines of thought, the proponents of abortion have reached one unexceptionable conclusion, that it would be a very good thing if every child were born "wanted," and one highly dubious conclusion, that the best way of bringing about this desirable state of affairs is to terminate the life of every child whose parents testify that he is *not* wanted.

The "wanted child" argument proceeds, however, on the basis of several slippery assumptions. One is the ethically questionable proposition that something as irrevocable as the death of a child can be balanced against something as chancy and changeable as the

[50]Prof. Shiden Inoue, unpublished manuscript entitled "Japan Must Stop the Practice of Abortion."

emotional state of a woman in early pregnancy. The other is the psychologically indefensible notion that parental attitudes during the customarily more or less tense and difficult period of pregnancy are a true reflection of what the attitudes of the same parents will be after the birth of their child. Dr. Joseph Donnelly has pointed to this aspect of the question.

Much has been said about the unwanted child and I would like to know exactly when a parent or a doctor decides that a child is unwanted. . . . There would be a considerable discrepancy about the answer the parents might give concerning whether a child was wanted or not, whether the poll was taken one month before conception, the night of conception, a night two months later when the mother is vomiting and the other two kids have the croup, or the day after delivery when the mother has the child in her arms. I am not sure when the child is unwanted and I am not sure that anyone else is either.[51]

Dr. Sim notes that the phenomenon of "not wanting" the child "very, very rarely persists after the fourth month of pregnancy."[52] Since, however, most abortions would presumably be performed before the end of the fourth month of pregnancy, it is apparent that if "not wanting" the child were to be accepted as grounds for abortion, this would lead to the destruction of children who, had they been

[51]Calderone, 103.
[52]Sim, "Psychiatric Indications for Abortion."

born, would have been accepted and loved by their parents.

It must, of course, be admitted that there will remain a small number of cases in which the parents, because of their emotional problems, will be permanently incapable of giving their children the love and acceptance necessary for their sound development. But the question is whether abortion is the appropriate solution in such circumstances. Here again one comes up against the bedrock issue of whether or not one believes that innocent human life can sometimes be directly destroyed in extreme circumstances. Those who do believe this will conclude that absolute and unalterable parental rejection of the child is one of those extreme, justifying circumstances. Those who do not, however, will note that there are other solutions to this problem besides abortion. Arrangements can, for example, be made for the adoption of children in such cases. Granted, adoptions will sometimes be difficult to arrange. But the difficulty is scarcely insoluble, given the will to solve it. The danger is that the quick, easy but ultimately inhumane solution of abortion will be preferred on grounds of expediency to the more difficult but also more humane solutions that are available.

The "wanted child" argument also has its darker side: the implications of an abortion for the relations between the parents and their living children. What impact does abortion have on the emotional security of children? Says one writer:

> Suppose they know that their mother had gotten rid of a baby because she didn't want it. Or suppose they know that mothers in general are like that. What does it do to the whole mother-child relationship? How does it affect a mother's attitude to her other children if she has once disposed of a baby in that way? What kind of persons result from growing up in that kind of atmosphere? How does our attitude toward everyone change if we judge a person's right to life by what his life does to our plans?
>
> These are the questions that the proponents of abortion as a form of birth control must answer. It is not only a baby's life, it is our whole social fabric which is placed in jeopardy by the present demand for virtually unlimited abortion. . . . If we lose the human faculty of imagination, if we grant humanity only to those whom we can see, and who look just like us, is there any solid foundation for human ethics? We will be back to the condition where the question that leaps to mind when we come face to face with another man is: "Can I kill him, or can he kill me?"[53]

[53]Julian Pleasants, "A Morality of Consequences," *Commonweal*, June 30, 1967.

V

Abortion Abroad

Detailed information about abortion in many parts of the world is hard to find or is nonexistent. The practice is, after all, illegal or closely restricted by legal limitations in most places. Nevertheless, in some countries which have lowered barriers against abortion, considerable information is available to show how the experiment has worked. It goes without saying, of course, that the experience of such diverse countries as Japan and Hungary is not totally relevant to the situation of the United States, where, one may assume, quite different attitudes toward childbirth and marriage are traditional. One cannot flatly say that "because such-and-such has happened in Japan," therefore the same thing is certain to happen in this country if similar laws on abortion are enacted here. But at the same time what has happened in other countries can scarcely be ignored in attempting to find out what might happen if the United States adopted liberalized abortion laws on a wide scale. At the very least it can be said that, where certain phenomena are repeated in a wide variety of countries which have tried liberalized abortion, the burden of proof must rest on those who would assert that the same things will not happen in the United States.

JAPAN

Staggering under the shock of defeat in war and the return of huge numbers of repatriates who had either emigrated or served in the armed forces, Japan in 1948 adopted a so-called Eugenic Protection Law embodying a national birth control program. The measure authorized voluntary and, in some cases, compulsory sterilization, as well as the public sale of contraceptives. It also legalized abortions on therapeutic or economic grounds. In 1952 the law was amended to make it even easier to obtain an abortion. "Practically any woman who so desires," says one writer, "can now have her pregnancy terminated."[1] The abortion policy, writes another, is one of "unhampered permissiveness."[2] Abortion is permitted up until the eighth month of pregnancy.[3]

The explanation for the relative ease with which Japan's policy of abortion on demand became law is interesting. Say Gebhard and his colleagues: "Since the Shinto and Buddhist religions are ethically blank on the subject of induced abortion, and since infanticide had in past centuries been an accepted

[1]Anthony Zimmerman, S.V.D., *Catholic Viewpoint on Overpopulation* (Garden City, N.Y., 1961), p. 68.
[2]Lawrence Lader, *Abortion* (New York, 1966), p. 117.
[3]Mary Steichen Calderone, M.D., ed., *Abortion in the United States* (New York, 1958), p. 200.

means of family limitation, it has not been difficult for legalized abortion to be readily adopted by the many who need a way to control family size."[4] More than 19,000 doctors have been authorized to perform abortions in Japan, and facilities for abortion have been set up in more than 800 health centers.

Japan is often cited as a country of large population and limited living space which has achieved success in its efforts at family limitation. The success, however, takes on a somewhat different aspect when it is realized that it is due largely to a huge growth in the number of abortions in the wake of the 1948 legislation. Despite official efforts to promote contraception and despite the sanction for sterilization, abortion has proved to be the "main factor" in the reduction of Japanese fertility.[5] Indeed, it is suggested that the ready availability of abortion is an obstacle to wider acceptance of contraception by married people.[6] In any case, the reduction in births has been dramatic. Japan's net reproduction rate dropped from 1.71 in 1947 to 0.89 in 1961. If this were to remain a permanent state of affairs one Japanese writer has pointed out, it would mean

[4]Paul H. Gebhard, Wardell B. Pomeroy, Clyde E. Martin, Cornelia V. Christenson, *Pregnancy, Birth and Abortion* (New York, 1958), p. 219.

[5]Richard M. Fagley, *The Population Explosion and Christian Responsibility* (New York, 1960), p. 84. Dr. Fagley is a Protestant Minister.

[6]*Abortion, An Ethical Discussion,* published for the Church Assembly Board for Social Responsibility by the Church Information Office (London, 1965), p. 10.

that the Japanese nation would "disappear from the face of the earth after some hundreds of years."[7]

In 1948 there were 246,104 registered abortions in Japan. By 1952 this figure had jumped to over a million, and in 1954 it reached a high of 1,170,143. More recently the annual number of registered abortions appears to have leveled off at about a million. Yet this is only part of the story, for the number of unregistered abortions is probably even larger. Estimates put the total of Japanese abortions, both registered and unregistered, at a minimum of 2.3 million per year and perhaps substantially higher.[8] The reasons why so many abortions go unreported in a country with notably lax laws on the subject include the desire of some doctors to avoid paying taxes on their fees for such operations, and the desire of parents to avoid the cost of otherwise compulsory mortuary services. What this means is "well over a 50 percent loss in all pregnancies."[9]

Although the Japanese abortion program is carried out under a "eugenic" law, the reasons for which abortions are sought are "usually economic, medical, or personal."[10] In one survey, more than eighty percent of a series of first abortions were sought on economic grounds; in another, the reasons "do not desire children" and "suffering from illness" were

[7]Prof. Shiden Inoue, manuscript entitled "Japan Must Stop the Practice of Abortion."
[8]National Catholic News Service, July 15, 1965.
[9]Gebhard et al., 219.
[10]*Ibid.*

equally balanced and together accounted for ninety percent of 5,200 abortion requests.[11]

How have the Japanese come to terms with this vast number of abortions? Evidence suggests a sense of uneasiness among part of the population and determined opposition in a smaller segment. A nationwide organization called the Movement to Treat Life Respectfully has been established to mobilize popular opposition to abortion. It numbers Christians, Buddhists, Shintoists and others among its members. Another group in 1964 collected 1,800,000 signatures on a petition condemning abortion and asking a tightening of the law. Neither the Japanese government nor the Japanese Family Planning Federation have encouraged abortion, and both have voiced concern over the swelling number of abortions. The Japanese Minister of Welfare has referred to abortion as an "evil practice" which is "eroding the physical and moral health of our nation."[12] The Ministry of Health has expressed concern that frequent abortions "necessarily produce undesirable effects upon the health of mothers."[13]

Similar reactions have cropped up in the Japanese popular press. The magazine *Josei Jishin* in March, 1962, carried a description of a run-of-the-mill abortion which, for all its somewhat melodramatic tone,

[11]*Ibid.*
[12]Quoted in Anthony Zimmerman, S.V.D., "An Abortion Explosion in Japan," *U.S. Catholic*, May, 1965.
[13]Quoted in Lader, 134.

is nevertheless symptomatic of a sense of alarm in at least some sectors of Japanese society.

> A steel forceps mangles and extracts a murky mass of bloody tissue. There it lies now, soft and quivering. But in it are hands and feet, even eyes and a nose well formed.
> Wash if you will. But washing won't help. That tiny bleeding object dyed in red is a human being, no doubt about it. It whimpers now with a voice like a little kitten. It is tossed into a dark corner by itself. The cries become faint; now it is dead. Its life was short, but a few moments. Another artificial termination of pregnancy has been completed.
> But this child had a father and a mother. A young lady is sleeping under heavy sedatives. Beside her pillow waits a young man; he is whistling, not knowing what else to do with himself.
> The two now tread the darkened hospital corridor in slippered feet. Her face is white as ashes. Now they have emerged into the sunlight outside. Neither one turns to look back. They hadn't even bothered to inquire whether it was a boy or a girl![14]

In a newspaper survey, twenty-six percent of the women who had had abortions said their health had been adversely affected, and another sixteen percent did not reply to the question. Such reactions, of course, involve a strong subjective factor. But the subjective factors, whatever their source, are quite real. If a woman *believes* she has suffered injury, by that fact alone she *has*. Another study of 1,712 legal abortions found slight or severe complications

[14]Quoted in Zimmerman, "An Abortion Explosion in Japan."

in forty-seven percent of all cases; the incidence of complications was somewhat higher in second and third abortions.[15] A study by the Mother and Child Health Section of the Welfare Ministry reported an eight percent incidence of complications.[16] One writer has summarized the post-abortion complications as follows:

> There are infections, chronic bleeding, tumors (sometimes cancer), menstrual disorders, upsetting of hormone balance, upsetting of the sympathetic nervous system. . . . [M]any complain that they cannot work as well as they used to, that they always feel tired, or have shoulder or hip cramps. Many have become sterile. One survey indicated that the incidence of extra-uterine pregnancies has increased by 400 percent since 1948 in Japan among women who have abortion experience.[17]

Apart from maternal health, abortion has had other harmful consequences in Japan. While many abortions are certainly performed in medically impeccable surroundings, other terminations of pregnancy take place in circumstances that can only be called degrading. One report found nonauthorized abortions being performed in an abortion clinic where patients were not required to make appointments, their names were not recorded, the price was fixed by haggling, and during the short time that instruments were soaked in an " 'antiseptic' solution," one pa-

[15]Gebhard et al., 219-20.
[16]*Ibid.*
[17]Zimmerman, "An Abortion Explosion in Japan."

tient wearing street clothes "crawled off and another patient crawled onto the blood encrusted table."[18] Gebhard and his associates, whose attitude can scarcely be called anti-abortion, refer to the "note of apology" on the part of Japanese spokesmen for the "docile cooperation" of Japanese women with the abortion program.[19] A Japanese representative at an international Planned Parenthood conference in Tokyo in 1955 said abortion "has become so popular in our country that it is almost a fashion."[20] Writers speak of an "abortion mood" in the country which has infected family and social life.[21] The easy availability of abortion is said to have undermined relationships between parents and children and to have fostered a selfish, pleasure-seeking and self-indulgent mentality. The Chief of the Children's Bureau of the Japanese Ministry of Welfare has stated that children raised in an "abortion age" feel a lack of parental love, and, as a result, turn to anti-social behavior and juvenile crime.[22] The abortion program has led to embarrassing incidents like that reported in March, 1967, by *Asahi Shimbun,* Japan's leading newspaper, in which a doctor sent letters to American hospitals and physicians offering them a ten percent commission on fees paid by American patients whom they referred to him for abortions.

[18]Quoted in Gebhard et al., 220-21 (footnote).
[19]Gebhard et al., 220.
[20]Quoted in Gebhard et al., 220.
[21]Zimmerman, "An Abortion Explosion in Japan."
[22]*Ibid.*

When asked by a client for assistance, he advised his correspondents, "simply let her fly to Tokyo and leave the rest to us. Satisfaction is guaranteed. Your introduction will be appreciated and 10 percent of the patient's payment for the operation will be paid to you as your introduction fee." When his promotional activities were publicized, the doctor apologized for his inadequate command of English but insisted he was not violating any law.[23]

Is abortion the key to Japan's postwar economic resurgence? The experts say no. Dr. Ryutaro Komiya of the Tokyo University School of Economics has stated that there is "scarcely any causal relation between birth-control [including abortion] and the present economic prosperity of Japan."[24] Japanese industrial capacity already existed from prewar and wartime years. So did an industrious and educated populace well prepared to feed the industrial machine. Indeed, concern is now being expressed lest abortion turn out to be a drag on the economy in the long run. Observers have warned of a looming shortage of high school and college graduates to fill the manpower needs of business and industry, a shortage that will be aggravated in the years ahead as the impact of the postwar abortion boom becomes more apparent.[25] And, as the composition of the population comes to include a larger proportion

[23]National Catholic News Service, March 9, 1967.
[24]Zimmerman, *Catholic Viewpoint*, 88.
[25]National Catholic News Service, July 15, 1965.

of elderly persons, the burden of supporting them will have to be borne by a shrinking number of young people. One study has described the situation as one of "serious imbalance in [Japan's] rapidly aging population."[26]

It is, however, generally agreed that there is no easy way of cutting down on Japanese abortions in the foreseeable future. The habit, once ingrained, is difficult to eradicate. Reviewing social problems created in Japan by the large-scale abortion program, a study published by a Church of England committee concludes:

> These reflections on Japan's experience, coming as they do from people who first accepted abortion as a desperate remedy for a desperate situation, must give pause to those who speak lightheartedly of "liberalizing the law" on abortion in this country. To build up a habit of mind which regards abortion lightly as an easy remedy for any adverse situation, personal or social, might be, in fact, to do people and society a grave disservice by addicting them to another social disease.[27]

SWEDEN

A Swedish law of 1734 made induced abortion a capital crime. In 1890 the penalty was reduced to two years at hard labor. In 1921 the punishment was reduced further and therapeutic abortion was accepted. Then in 1938 a new law was enacted establishing sociomedical, humanitarian and eugenic

[26]*Abortion, An Ethical Discussion,* 11.
[27]*Abortion, An Ethical Discussion,* 54.

grounds for abortion. The law was liberalized still further in 1946 by an amendment permitting abortion when there is a likelihood of "foreseeable maternal weaknesses." The latter category, it is explained, was intended to provide for "such future contingencies in the mother's life as the strain of giving birth to and caring for the new child."[28] The legislation authorized abortion when, "taking account of a woman's conditions of life and other circumstances, there are reasons for foreseeing that her physical or mental capacity would be seriously affected by the birth of a child and the care it entails."

The Swedish abortion program is of interest on several counts, not least because of the prediction that it will provide the model for the initial American abortion "reform." Thus Lawrence Lader, describing the Scandinavian approach to abortion as "an eminently rational system, attuned to the humanitarian instincts and moderate planning that have made these nations a model of social progress," foresees that "the first American states to adopt abortion reform will undoubtedly turn to the Scandinavian model."[29]

Legal abortion is not ordinarily permitted in Sweden beyond the twentieth week of pregnancy, although in exceptional cases it is allowed up to the twenty-fourth week. Most applications for abor-

[28]Gebhard et al., 222.
[29]Lader, 117.

tion are passed on by a committee consisting of a physician, a lay person (preferably a woman) and the Chief of the Bureau for Social Psychiatry of the Royal Medical Board.

Sweden is widely regarded as a haven of easy abortion. As a matter of fact, however, a rather conscientious effort is made to enforce the legal norms for abortion, and a substantial number of requests are refused. In 1962, for example, when 2,600 legal abortions were granted, thirty-nine percent of all petitions were rejected.[30] The pattern in Sweden has been one of a large upsurge in legal abortions after the initial liberalization of the law, followed by a decline in the total as the norms were more strictly enforced. Thus, in 1939 legal abortions totalled 439; in 1957 they reached a high of 6,328; and in 1962, as noted, they had dropped off to 2,600.[31]

A feature of the Swedish program is the coupling of abortion with sterilization, especially in cases where the abortion is not the woman's first. In the years 1946-1951, more than twenty-five percent of all legal abortions were accompanied by sterilization.[32] Reporting this, Gebhard and his colleagues add: "Since the fatality ratio in the double operation was nearly four times as great as it was when only an abortion was performed, this seems a fairly

[30]*Abortion, An Ethical Discussion,* 55.
[31]*Ibid.*
[32]Gebhard et al., 223.

drastic measure to cut the future abortion figure."[33]

The Swedish experience has particular relevance for this discussion because of the light it sheds on the familiar argument that making it easier to obtain a legal abortion cuts the ground from under illegal abortionists and reduces the number of unsanctioned operations. The thrust of this argument is that it would "surely be right to rescue abortion from this distressing guilt-ridden atmosphere which . . . causes it to proliferate, and give it a cover of legality and reasonable justification; the result would be a cleansing of the social atmosphere and a reawakening of a sense of responsibility."[34]

Strange to say, however, Sweden's experience has been the reverse. Though legal abortions are easier to obtain and their number has risen sharply since 1938, it is generally admitted that they are equaled or exceeded by the number of illegal abortions. In 1939 Sweden recorded 107,380 live births and 439 legal abortions. In 1955 there were 107,305 live births and 4,562 legal abortions. The "general opinion" is "undoubtedly that criminal abortion has increased alongside legal abortion" in Sweden.[35] A

[33]*Ibid.*

[34]Stanislas de Lestapis, S. J., "Birth Control as a Population Remedy: Contraception and Some of Its Effects on Society," in Arthur McCormick, ed., *Christian Responsibility and World Poverty* (Westminster, Md., 1963), 69-70. Father de Lestapis does not, of course, share the point of view expressed here but only seeks to give it voice in order to analyze it.

[35]Dr. Jean Sutter, quoted in de Lestapis, 70.

Swedish delegate to a Planned Parenthood conference in Tokyo in 1955 said the number of criminal
abortions had registered "a steady increase since the
law came into force" and added: "This increase is
due to the fact that the possibility of terminating
pregnancy has become a topic of conversation, with
the result that the idea of abortion is generally accepted among our people."[36] As another source
puts it: "[I]llicit abortion continues because women
who are determined to have it either will not face
the tribunal and its requirements, or will not accept
from it a negative decision."[37] Gebhard and his
associates note the suggestion that legalized abortion has in fact not touched the illegal abortions at
all: all legalization has done is to create a new
"clientele" for abortion among a group of women
who are "quite separate from those who would
resort to illegal abortion."[38] The same thought is
developed in the following passage:

> Various theories have been advanced, the more in-
> teresting being of a sociological order. Hegnelius
> (1954) and Simon (1954), for instance, admit that
> criminal abortions of the old type have not been
> touched by the new law. In fact it has merely created
> a new demand for abortion, by producing a new
> mentality in the unintentionally pregnant woman, who
> has gradually accustomed herself to the idea of getting
> rid of her child without encumbrance. Axel Westman,

[36]Quoted in George A. Kelly, *Birth Control and Catholics*
(Garden City, N. Y., 1963), 110-11.
[37]*Abortion, An Ethical Discussion*, 55.
[38]Gebhard et al., 224.

who could not be suspected of anti-neo-Malthusianism, refers to a tendency for the idea to catch on from one woman to another.[39]

Some estimates of the number of illegal abortions put the total at 12,000 per year.[40] Even one who disagrees with Lawrence Lader's proposed solution —abortion on demand—can accept his diagnosis: "The very fact that the system is tightly controlled, and many cases rejected, makes it impossible to cut deeply into underworld abortion."[41]

Recently it was reported that some Swedish women have gone to Poland, said to be the easiest country in Europe in which to obtain an abortion, for operations which they could not obtain under the relatively permissive laws of their own country.[42] This suggests the extent to which the idea of abortion has "caught on" in Sweden: the attitude is one which regards abortion as a woman's natural right and prerogative. It suggests, too, that one of the likely consequences of "moderate" abortion reform legislation is to encourage in large numbers of people an attitude of across-the-board acceptance of abortion. The end result of moderate legislation may not be far different from a program of frank abortion on demand. Thus Sweden's "middle way," proposed as a "model" for the United States.

[39]Sutter, quoted in de Lestapis, 70.
[40]Lader, 120.
[41]*Ibid.*
[42]*The New York Times*, February 14, 1965.

DENMARK

A similar pattern of "moderate" abortion reform legislation followed by a persistent and substantial incidence of illegal abortion emerges in Denmark, which in 1939 put into operation a law providing for a broad interpretation of therapeutic abortion. Denmark had its parallel to Britain's *Bourne* case, too, the 1935 trial of Dr. J. H. Leunbach, who performed abortions in a clinic for working-class women, using a paste injection. Dr Leunbach was first acquitted but later sentenced to three months in prison and disqualified from practicing medicine for five years.

An important feature of the Danish abortion program is the role played by the Mothers Aid Organization. Where abortion is sought on grounds other than danger to the mother's life or health resulting from illness, certification must be provided that the woman has received information about alternatives from a Mothers Aid Center. Vera Skalts and Magna Norgaard, officials of the Mothers Aid Center in Copenhagen, explain that this is because "in those cases where the indication for abortion was not purely medical, but rather where social, economic, familial, or personal reasons were prevailing, an attempt should always be made to solve these problems and avoid abortion."[43] It is interesting that in a recent symposium on abortion, Skalts and Norgaard

[43]Vera Skalts and Magna Norgaard, "Abortion Legislation in Denmark," in David T. Smith, ed., *Abortion and the Law* (Cleveland, 1967), 150.

repeatedly stress the undesirability of abortion and the necessity for taking all means to dissuade women from it. Thus, "legal abortion is a highly deplorable step," and "as a preferable alternative to abortion, constructive help and support should be provided to women in unwanted pregnancy so as to encourage them to carry through their pregnancy."[44] They note further that it is the experience of Mothers Aid that "a number of women in an originally unwanted pregnancy can be encouraged to change their minds and carry through their pregnancy; the Centers are convinced that a much greater number ought to be helped and could be helped if satisfactory means of help and support were available."[45]

The first Danish law, which came into effect in 1939, provided three indications for abortion. These were medical and sociomedical, when pregnancy was judged a serious danger to the woman's life or health; "ethical," when the pregnancy was the result of criminal acts; and hereditary, where there was serious danger that the child would suffer severe hereditary illness or impairment. A fourth category was added under the Pregnancy Act of 1956—abortion where the woman was judged unfit to take proper care of her child. Of the latter indication for abortion, Skalts and Norgaard say that "in principle, it is a social indication, it being the interests of the child, not the woman herself, that are safeguarded."[46]

[44]Skalts and Norgaard, 146.
[45]Skalts and Norgaard, 168.
[46]Skalts and Norgaard, 156.

It applies, among other things, to cases in which the mother is mentally retarded or mentally ill. Commenting on this indication for abortion, Dr. Henrik Hoffmeyer, Assistant Superintendent of the State Psychiatric Hospital, Copenhagen, notes that it is "somewhat humiliating" to the woman in question.[47]

Dr. Hoffmeyer also observes that the medical indication is the most commonly used. It includes, he says, "convention conflicts," "stress syndromes," and "stress syndrome of housewives."[48] The first situation arises when the pregnancy or the expected child "provokes a conflict between the woman and the conventions of the social group to which she belongs," as in cases of illegitimacy among married women. The second is a "more or less chronic condition existing before the pregnancy" and most commonly found among married women who have several children and suffer from such difficulties as poor housing or marital problems. As for the "stress syndrome of housewives," it occurs in two forms: one "dominated by social, financial, and housing problems," the other appearing in middle-class women who are "not directly threatened by social destitution due to the pregnancy, but who are motivated to seek an abortion through the fear of a reduction in their standard of living."

[47]Henrik Hoffmeyer, M.D., "Medical Aspects of the Danish Legislation on Abortion," in Smith, 195.
[48]Hoffmeyer, 183-92.

The Danish law provides that abortion be performed before the sixteenth week of pregnancy when the grounds are ethical, hereditary or possible defect. There are, however, no time limits on medical or sociomedical abortions, and in urgent cases abortion "is possible at any time during the pregnancy."[49] In 1963, legal abortions in Denmark totalled 3,970. Two-thirds of the applicants for legal abortion in 1963-64 were married, twenty-four percent were unmarried, and ten percent were divorced, separated or widowed.[50]

There is, as Skalts and Norgaard point out, considerable emphasis in the Danish system on getting the abortion applicant to delay her decision and reconsider her request in the light of counseling and information on the availability of services. They note that it is "useful for the woman to have time to reflect and reconsider the decision to have the abortion performed, since the initial decision may have been made when the feelings of panic and depression during the first few months of her pregnancy were present."[51] Dr. Hoffmeyer observes that the depression states of early pregnancy are "rarely very deep" and when an application for illegal abortion is rejected "the panic normally declines."[52] Suicide threats or "superficial suicidal acts" are sometimes made, "but most often these are a part of the

49Hoffmeyer, 196.
50Skalts and Norgaard, 161.
51Skalts and Norgaard, 159-60.
52Hoffmeyer, 183.

appeal for legal abortion"; the women in whom the suicide danger is real "seldom seek the aid of a doctor or the Mothers Aid Center."[53] Other women, Dr. Hoffmeyer adds, turn at once to illegal abortion because they realize that the delay might result in the pregnancy's passing the point "where the emotional balance is normally changed in favor of the baby." He concludes:

> The assessment of the danger to life or health cannot be based only upon an observation of the present emotional state. The immediate reaction to an unwanted pregnancy is highly dependent upon personality traits influencing the sensitivity and reactivity and tells very little about the ability that the woman might have for overcoming her conflict and for coping with the situation in the long run.[55]

In sum, Dr. Hoffmeyer holds that restrictions and a measure of delay in handling applications for abortion are valuable.

> . . . [I]t is felt that unlimited abortions, or abortions on "social" grounds, would expose some women to a danger, namely, that they could be subjected to pressure from the husband, the fiancé, or other relatives. Moreover, the common, temporary mental depression of the first months of pregnancy certainly would induce some women to apply for an abortion which they later would regret.[56]

[53]Hoffmeyer, 184.
[54]Hoffmeyer, 185.
[55]Hoffmeyer, 191.
[56]Hoffmeyer, 204.

In the wake of the Danish abortion reform, illegal abortions have not declined and probably have increased in number. With births running about 80,000 per year, and legal abortions totalling about 4,000, the number of illegal abortions has been estimated at 12,000 to 15,000.[57] Other estimates run even higher.

A movement is now underway in Denmark to introduce legal abortion on demand. In September, 1967, Minister of Justice K. Axel Nielsen, responding to pressure from Liberals, Social Democrats and Socialists, established a special committee to examine the whole issue. The proposal for abortion on demand has been attacked by Lutheran Bishop K. Westergaard Madsen, who wrote in the daily *Kristeligt Dagblad:*

> We hear that about 20,000 illegal abortions take place each year in Denmark. This is a serious situation and demands a remedy. But to find a solution in legalizing abortion is to ignore the fact that abortion brings the end of a life. It is superficial to talk only about the man's or the woman's rights. There is another person involved, the unborn child, who also has rights.[58]

HUNGARY

Shortly before the unsuccessful revolution of 1956, a drastic population limitation program was undertaken in Hungary, including a sharp rise in the

[57]Hoffmeyer, 200.
[58]National Catholic News Service, February 10, 1967.

number of abortions. The result, in the estimation of a Hungarian emigré source, has been a "population catastrophe unprecedented in its [Hungary's] history."[59] Where, between 1950 and 1952, abortions had averaged about 1,700 annually, in less than a decade after the 1956 uprising the abortion total was a million and a half. In terms of the United States population, this would have meant 28.5 million abortions in the same period. The primary factor in this situation is a 1956 law authorizing abortion on demand.

The law provides that requests for abortion be directed to a three-member committee whose chairman is a doctor. The committee, however, can function only as a rubber stamp, for it must approve the abortion "if the applicant insists."[60] Andras Klinger of the Hungarian Central Office of Statistics reports that in 1964 less than four percent of all abortions were performed because of illness; the rest were "on the basis of other (social or family) causes."[61] A survey in 1964 of women who had undergone abortion found that nearly a third sought termination of pregnancy simply on the grounds that they already had enough children.[62] The Hungarian social insurance system covers abortions performed

[59]The American Hungarian Society, *S.O.S. From Hungary*, P. O. Box 162, Gracie Station, New York.

[60]Andras Klinger, "Abortion Programs," in Bernard Berelson, ed., *Family Planning and Population Programs: A Review of World Developments* (Chicago, 1966), p. 466.

[61]*Ibid.*

[62]Klinger, 467.

because of illness. In cases of abortion on non-medical grounds, the applicant or her husband must pay hospital costs for the first three days, but thereafter the woman is entitled to free services. This means, Klinger notes, that the average woman who undergoes an abortion must pay 360 forints, about $16, which represents approximately one-fifth of average monthly earnings, a sum which "does not cause any difficulty to applicants and does not hinder them from applying for permission to interrupt unwanted pregnancies."[63]

Radio Budapest reported in January, 1963, that an abortion was performed in Hungary every three minutes. Abortions now occur at the rate of about 200,000 per year. In 1964, according to Klinger, the abortion rate was ninety-one per 1,000 married women aged fifteen to forty-nine; it was also 140 percent of the live birthrate—that is, abortions exceeded births by forty percent.[64] Many women have repeated abortions. Between 1960 and 1964 the percentage of women undergoing their third or higher abortion increased from 25.5 percent to 31.4 percent; women having their fifth or higher abortion accounted for 7.5 percent of the total in 1964, compared with 5.2 percent in 1960.[65] This suggests "an increasing tendency among women who resort to this method of birth limitation in the first place to

[63]Klinger, 469.
[64]Klinger, 475.
[65]Klinger, 471.

continue to rely on its use."[66] Between 1960 and 1964 there was also a "pronounced" increase in the number of childless women, and women with only one child, undergoing abortion. Childless married women who had experienced abortion increased sixty-four percent in this period, and the rate per 1,000 was almost as high among women with one child as among women with two children.[67] There is as well an "increasing trend" toward induced abortion among young, unmarried women; nearly 7,000—two percent—of the unmarried women under the age of twenty sought induced abortion in 1964.[68]

As in Japan, public health problems have made their appearance.

> Many thousand Hungarian women have had their health permanently impaired by surgical abortions. Leading medical authorities of the nation started sounding the alarm years ago over the abnormally high number of premature births, spontaneous abortions and increasing sterility among women, and the increase of retarded children born to mothers who had surgically interrupted pregnancies. A . . . conference sponsored by the University of Medical Science in Pécs made public irrefutable statistics proving that in Hungary: a) the ratio of premature births almost doubled, b) more than half the retarded children were born prematurely and c) every third woman who became sterile had previously undergone surgical abortion. The participating doctors all agreed that the regime's abortion edict should be drastically revised.[69]

[66]*Ibid.*
[67]*Ibid.*
[68]Klinger, 473.
[69]*S.O.S. From Hungary.*

The mortality rate from abortion in Hungary is said to be quite low, largely because abortion is permitted only up to the twelfth week of pregnancy. But, says Klinger, "the complications of induced abortion are . . . more significant." In 1964, of every 1,000 women undergoing abortion, 1.3 suffered perforation of the uterus; 8.5 "feverish conditions"; and 16.4 hemorrhage.[70] Declaring that induced abortion "cannot be viewed as a proper and suitable means of birth control," Klinger concludes that "its deleterious effect on health is sufficient reason to change the present-day situation."[71] Singling out the problem of premature births, he notes that their incidence increases with the number of abortions a woman has experienced. Thus, a 1964 study showed the ratio of premature births among women who had no induced abortions to be ten percent; for women with one induced abortion, it was fourteen percent; with two induced abortions, sixteen percent; and with three or more induced abortions, twenty-one percent.[72] He concludes:

> Thus, the impact of premature birth on infant mortality and on the mental and physical development of the child is connected with the frequency of abortions. These relationships have not yet been studied in detail, but it is clear that induced abortion plays an important role in the development of a later child. It might be noted that in Budapest, where the fre-

[70]Klinger, 475.
[71]Klinger, 476.
[72]Klinger, 474.

quency of induced abortion is highest, the frequency of premature births is very high.[73]

Concern over the consequences of abortion has led to a free-wheeling debate over the national policy. Leading Hungarian authors and intellectuals have sharply criticized the mentality of easy abortion and warned of the dangers to the nation. Newspapers and magazines have criticized the prevalent antichild attitude; even a nightclub act has used as its theme the question, "A car or a child, which is more important?"[74] The one-child family is now a reality; indeed, the average now is .86 children per couple.[75] János Kodolányi, described as the dean of Hungarian writers, declared in the literary magazine *Kortars*, "No woman has the right to destroy her unborn child. If she does, she destroys herself and ultimately contributes to the destruction of her people."[76] A Communist writer, Károly Jobbágy, who favored the legalization of abortions in 1956, wrote in the February, 1964, issue of the publication *Elet és Irodalom:*

> I would not have believed that, scarcely eight years [after the legalization of abortions], we would be looking at this freedom with doubt, struggling with the monstrous possibility of the extinction of our nation. . . . The fact is that the Hungarian nation is growing weaker. An unexpected world crisis, an un-

[73]*Ibid.*
[74]Lader, 126.
[75]*Ibid.*
[76]S.O.S. *From Hungary.*

known epidemic may come when strong peoples will survive, while smaller and weaker ones will fall. And then our history and our literature will be but a memory, stuff for scholars.[77]

The writer Pál Szabó commented in *Szabad Föld* that it should be "clear to everyone" that abortion means not only the extinction of countless infant lives, but an impairment of the lives of those who continue to live.[78] "A life without tomorrow," he explained, "can no longer be called life." Szabó advocated an end to abortion on demand and its replacement by a more wholesome family planning program, as well as an adequate nationwide nursery system and improvement in the social conditions of working women. In a recent poem Gyula Illyés pushed the logic of abortion to its ultimate conclusion: "If today we kill off the unborn children because as unproductive elements they would burden our economy, tomorrow, using the same morbid logic, we could liquidate the older generations as well."[79]

All this has led the American Hungarian Society to warn that the nation faces an "ethnic Stalingrad" in the years ahead.[80] A shrinking number of young, productive people will be called on to support an abnormally large proportion of aged persons. And a lack of manpower could mean a drastic setback

[77]*Ibid.*
[78]*Ibid.*
[79]*Ibid.*
[80]*Ibid.*

for business, industry and agriculture in the nineteen-eighties.

THE SOVIET UNION

The Soviet Union has reversed its policy on abortion twice in the past fifty years, swinging from extreme permissiveness to extreme restrictiveness, and then back again to permissiveness. Ideological, economic and medical reasons all seem to have played a part in these sharp reversals, although official explanations offer less than a total clarification of the conflicting policies.

Free, legal abortion in government hospitals was introduced in 1920. The ideological motivation was that this was part of the new Soviet society's program to emancipate women and give them equal rights with men by not obliging them to bear unwanted children. Other reasons seem to have been the desire to reduce illegal abortion, and economic considerations: smaller families were deemed an asset as the country moved into a period of intensive industrialization in which married women were needed to swell the working force.[81]

In the next fifteen years the number of legal abortions soared, increasing fourfold by 1925 and ten times again by 1935. The abortions were most commonly performed in government clinics or "abortoria," and the technique has been described as an

[81]Gebhard et al., 216; Lader, 121.

"assembly-line approach."[82] Some foreign doctors who observed these methods at the time expressed doubts about them. One spoke of abortions being "somewhat hurriedly done, at an eight-minute interval of time"; another reported eight abortions in a Moscow abortorium "performed within a two-hour period"; another referred to the "gruesome" efficiency of the abortoria.[83] Official reports claimed an extremely low incidence of deaths and complications. One reason, however, may be that the abortion patient was discharged from the abortorium soon after the operation, with follow-up care left to regular hospitals; such complications as occurred thus did not generally find their way onto the records of the abortoria.[84]

Nevertheless, there is evidence that Soviet doctors often opposed abortions and sought to dissuade women from having them. It may be that the opposition of the medical profession was one of the factors leading to the reversal of policy in 1936.[85] In any event, by the early nineteen-thirties warnings about the undesirable physical and emotional consequences of even legal abortion began to crop up in Russian medical literature. In June, 1936, the government outlawed abortion, except on strict medical grounds.

In addition to medical reasons, other considerations of a social, economic and political nature may

[82]Lader, 121.
[83]Gebhard et al., 217; Lader 121.
[84]Gebhard et al., 217 (footnote).
[85]Gebhard et al., 218.

have dictated this move. It has been suggested that Soviet leaders had become alarmed at the implications of the abortion program for the national population, in view of the impending conflict with Nazi Germany.[86] Another explanation is that the ban on abortion was part of "a larger crack-down on the revolutionary enthusiasm of the old Bolsheviks," corresponding to other measures taken by Stalin to reverse social and educational policies associated with the early days of the revolution.[87]

In November, 1955, however, the pendulum swung once again and the government reinstituted a program of permissive legalized abortion. Again, clear explanations are hard to come by. The official declaration was that Soviet women were now sufficiently conscientious to be entrusted with such decisions themselves. Another suggestion is that the action represented a response by the regime to public demand for some of the material amenities of life: "The average Soviet couple was desperately eager to delay another child in exchange for a private bedroom or a new suit."[88]

In any case, the Soviet abortion rate is said now to be extremely high, among the highest in the world. Estimates of the annual abortion total range between 2,000,000 and nearly 6,000,000.[89] Indeed, there

[86]Lader, 122.
[87]*Ibid.*
[88]*Ibid.*
[89]Lader, 123.

are indications that the high incidence of abortion has provoked renewed alarm among the authorities. It has been reported that Soviet doctors are no longer performing abortions unless a woman already has two children or unless there are compelling social reasons for termination of pregnancy. (Rape and overcrowding are rated on a par in this category.)[90]

Among married women, the incidence of abortion is three times as great among working wives as among non-working wives.[91] Demand for abortions is most common among urban married women. Reasons for which abortion is sought include lack of housing, lack of child care facilities or simple opposition to childbearing at that particular time.[92]

Abortion is also reported to be extremely common among female university students. One estimate was that forty percent of the undergraduate women at the Moscow State University had experienced abortions. Of this estimate a female student is reported to have remarked: "Don't be so naive. The real figure is probably closer to eighty percent."[93] Abortion at the university medical clinic costs about a dollar.

Official government policy on population matters appears to be rather ambivalent, with contraception permitted, but by no means pushed. In this situation the program of large-scale abortion seems likely to

[90]Paul Ferris, *The Nameless: Abortion in Britain Today* (London, 1966), p. 166.
[91]Lader, 122.
[92]Lader, 123.
[93]Quoted in Lader, 123.

continue for some time to come. As one writer puts it, "legalized abortion rather than contraception will undoubtedly satisfy the government's aims for the foreseeable future."[94]

[94]Lader, 125.

VI

Abortion and the Christian Tradition

In Rome at the beginning of the Christian era abortion and infanticide were common and widely accepted practices of long standing. Roman abortion arose from "luxurious and dissipated living among the wealthy and the powerful, inspired by idleness, love of comfort and female vanity."[1] Laws were adopted at one time or another in an effort to curb the practice. But their success, at least until Christianity became powerful in the secular state, was limited and their motivation ambiguous. Some measures against dealers in abortifacient potions and aphrodisiacs were apparently designed to shield adult health rather than preserve fetal life against attack.[2] Other laws punishing women who underwent abortions without the consent of their husbands were intended as protection for the rights of the

[1]Eugene Quay, "Justifiable Abortion," *The Georgetown Law Journal,* Vol. 49, No. 2 (Winter 1960), 173-256; Vol. 49, No. 3 (Spring 1961), 395-538. Page 420.

[2]John T. Noonan, Jr., *Contraception: A History of Its Treatment by the Catholic Theologians and Canonists* (Cambridge, Mass., 1965), p. 27.

156

deprived father rather than the child.[3] In general, the Roman attitude toward fetal and infant life merited the description "strikingly callous."[4]

Many classical Roman writers refer to abortion. Roman literature contains stern condemnations of the practice. Even Ovid, scarcely notable for his high standards of morality, speaks harshly of abortion:

> She who first plucked forth the tender life deserved to die in the warfare she began. Can it be that, to spare your bosom the reproach of lines, you would scatter the tragic sands of deadly combat? If vicious ways like this had found favour with mothers of olden time, the race of mortal men would have perished from the earth. . . .
>
> Why cheat the full vine of the growing cluster, and pluck with ruthless hand the fruit yet in the green? What is ripe will fall of itself—let grow what has once become quick; a life is no slight reward for a short delay. Ah, women, why will you thrust and pierce with the instrument, and give dire poisons to your children yet unborn?[5]

Juvenal, a far sterner moralist, sounds the same theme:

> Rarely does a gilded bed contain a woman lying-in:

[3]*Ibid.* The Emperors Severus and Antoninus decreed exile for a woman who procured abortion, "for it may be considered dishonorable for a woman to deprive her husband of children with impunity."
[4]Noonan, 85.
[5]*Amores,* II. Loeb edition (1914).

so potent are the arts and drugs of her that can insure barrenness, and for bribes kill men while yet unborn.[6]

Thus from the very start the new religion of Christianity was confronted with a society in which abortion was frequent and notorious. Its reaction was quick and to the point: the practice was condemned without qualification. The *Didache,* the earliest known Christian writing (it was composed between 65 and 80 A.D.), includes under the "second commandment of the teaching" the precept, "Thou shalt not procure abortion." This has continued to be Christian teaching for nearly 2,000 years.

In the second century, Christian condemnation of abortion was expressed by the "Letter of Barnabas" and by the lawyer Minucius Felix. In the third century the same doctrine was repeated by Tertullian ("He is man who is future man"[7]) and Cyprian; in the fourth century by the council of Elvira (a local Spanish council) and the council of Ancyra.

The canons of St. Basil, which became the basis of legislation in the Eastern Church, condemned without qualification women who procure abortion and provided the same penalty as Ancyra, ten years' penance. In the Western Church, St. Jerome described as a parricide the mother who sought an abortion. St. Augustine, in a famous passage which,

[6]*Satires,* VI, in Evans and Gifford, *The Satires of Juvenal, Persius, Sulpicia and Lucilius* (2nd ed., 1882).
[7]Quoted in Noonan, 91.

more than a millenium later, was to be recalled by
Pope Pius XI in his encyclical *Casti Connubii*, wrote:

> Sometimes this lustful cruelty, or cruel lust, comes
> to this, that they even procure poisons of sterility, and,
> if these do not work, extinguish and destroy the fetus
> in some way in the womb, preferring that their off-
> spring die before it lives, or if it was already alive in
> the womb to kill it before it was born. Assuredly if
> both husband and wife are like this, they are not
> married, and if they were like this from the beginning
> they come together not joined in matrimony but in
> seduction.[8]

This remained the Christian position throughout
the Middle Ages and Renaissance. In 1588 Pope Sixtus V, in the bull *Effraenatam*, proclaimed abortion
to be murder and invoked the penalty of excommunication for it. The stern Sixtus' bull was, however,
revoked in large part by his successor, Gregory XIV;
although he nevertheless retained the penalty of
excommunication in the case of abortion of a forty-
day-old fetus.

The nineteenth century witnessed a faltering in
the teaching of some theologians, reacting to arguments in favor of therapeutic abortion. It was said,
for example, that in some cases the fetus might be
killed as an "unjust aggressor" threatening the life
of the mother; that abortion was not direct killing
but the mere "removal" of the child, whose death
was tolerated according to the norms of the prin-

[8]*Marriage and Concupiscence.* Quoted in Noonan, 136.

ciple of "double effect"; that in a "conflict of rights,"
the mother's right, supposedly the stronger of the
two, should prevail; or that the child should be regarded as "yielding voluntarily" his right to life in
favor of the mother.[9]

Such theories were condemned by the Vatican's
Congregation of the Holy Office in a series of declarations in 1884, 1889, 1895 and 1898. This teaching
was solemnly repeated by Pius XI in *Casti Connubii*
and by Pius XII in several statements.

In passing, it is worth noting an action by Pope
Pius IX in 1869, providing the penalty of excommunication for persons guilty of abortion at any stage.
Excommunication, as noted, had previously been
invoked only when the abortion occurred after the
fortieth day of pregnancy. It is sometimes asserted
in popular pro-abortion tracts that this canonical
provision by Pius shows that the Catholic Church,
prior to 1869, did not consider abortion to be wrong.
However, as John Noonan has pointed out, this
argument "confuses a change in discipline with a
change in belief."[10] Pius' action in instituting the
penalty of excommunication for abortion at any
stage does not mean that prior to that time the
Church did not condemn all abortions; it means

[9]T. Lincoln Bouscaren, *Ethics of Ectopic Operations*, 2nd
ed., revised (Milwaukee, 1944), p. 5.
[10]John T. Noonan, Jr., in *The Reasons Against Abortion*,
statements before the Codes and Health Committees of the
New York Legislature, February 3, 8 and 10, 1967, distributed by the New York State Catholic Welfare Committee (mimeographed).

simply that up to that point the penalty of excommunication was not invoked in all cases. "Similarly, the Church in some ages excommunicated the killers of adult human beings, and sometimes did not excommunicate them. This variety of sanction does not mean that the Church ever approved or permitted the killing of adult human beings, but that discipline varied."[11]

It would of course be false to claim that all Christian churches today join in condemning abortion, although there was certainly unanimity on this point in the past. Many non-Catholic churchmen defend abortion in certain circumstances. The National Council of Churches stated in 1961 that the destruction of fetal life is permitted when "the health or life of the mother is at stake."[12] In 1958 the Anglican Church's Lambeth Conference, while declaring that Christians reject abortion "in the strongest terms," nevertheless went on to make room for the practice "at the dictate of strict and undeniable medical necessity."[13]

Among serious religious thinkers who presently

[11]*Ibid.*

[12]Quoted in Robert F. Drinan, S. J., "Contemporary Protestant Thinking," *America*, December 9, 1967.

[13]Curiously enough, the same statement adds just two sentences later, in apparent contradiction, that "the sacredness of life is, in Christian eyes, an absolute which should not be violated." If the sacredness of life is really an "absolute," it is difficult to see how it can properly be violated, even in the name of "strict and undeniable medical necessity." Or is one to assume a category of things which are only relatively absolute?

defend abortion, the argument is generally couched in terms of so-called situation ethics. A complete analysis and critique of this ethical approach is obviously outside the scope of this study. Briefly, however, it may be said that situationism argues that moral decisions, rather than being based on universal moral laws, should instead be derived from the particular situation in which a particular individual finds himself. It holds, in the language of one of its chief exponents, Dr. Joseph Fletcher, Professor of Christian Ethics at the Episcopal Theological School in Cambridge, Massachusetts, that "really, there is no act that is intrinsically good or evil. The morality of any act depends on the circumstances under which it is performed — the motives of those involved."[14]

However, although situationism postulates the absence of moral absolutes, situationists regularly end by embracing one or another absolute as the norm by which the morality of actions is to be judged. In most cases this absolute norm is love, charity or some variation. A Catholic situationist, the Most Rev. Francis Simons, describes the "good of mankind" as "the very basis of morality" in an article arguing for the morality, in some circumstances, of abortion and other actions generally condemned by Christian moral tradition.[15]

[14]Quoted in David Lowe, *Abortion and the Law* (New York, 1966), p. 95.

[15]Most Rev. Francis Simons, "The Catholic Church and the New Morality," *Cross Currents*, Vol. XVI, No. 4 (Fall 1966), pp. 429-45.

Without entering into a full-scale discussion of situationism, several remarks deserve to be made. First, on a prosaic but extremely practical level, it should be recognized that setting "love" as the sole norm of morality simply leaves too much opportunity for self-deception. Anyone with even a smattering of psychoanalytic sophistication must realize the extreme difficulty—bordering on practical impossibility in many cases—of an individual's knowing the real motives behind his actions. A morality which proposes that virtually anything can be done, provided only it is done out of "love," predicates a degree of self-awareness which few, if any people, possess. Furthermore, it should be evident that anyone who imagines he has "love" as love is understood in the Christian tradition is deeply confused about the true content of that virtue. The model of Christian "love" is, after all, nothing less than the Trinity, the perfect instance of complete unity and complete individuality. To suppose that the poor, on-again, off-again feelings of benevolence that we experience are true embodiments of this "love" is self-delusion. Genuine Christian "love" is something toward which Christians must aspire and struggle throughout their lives; it is not something which they already possess fully and which therefore they can use as the sole norm for determining the morality of their actions. Nor is it appropriate to fall back on the New Testament, and say that Christ's moral teaching was solely based on "love." Christ does indeed say that "love" summarizes the whole of His teaching, but the New Testament also contains a number of quite specific moral imperatives by Christ. St. Augustine also agrees that there is but one principal virtue, charity. But this central virtue of love "manifests itself in four ways as the cardinal virtues: as temperance, which is love keeping one's self whole and incorrupt for God; as justice, which is love rightly using all things in the service of God; as fortitude, which is love easily bearing anything for God; as prudence, which is love correctly distinguishing those things that help man reach God from those that would impede him."[16] As one author puts it:

> The "new morality" way of thinking forgets the place of "the natural order," the "order of creation," or the natural law, in the teaching of Christ Himself and in the doctrine of St. Paul. It ignores the place of the Decalogue in both the Old and the New Testament. It overlooks the fact that the Ten Commandments are always presented in the Bible in the context of the Covenant whereby God calls His People to be faithful to His Love. They are the People of God's response in the dialogue of love in which God has spoken the first word. They present the pattern of life which alone is becoming to a chosen, consecrated, priestly people. The words of Christ, "If you love Me, keep My commandments"; and the answering words of St. Paul, "love is the fulfillment of the law," provided the true scriptural relationship between law and love.[17]

[16]G. J. Dalcourt, "Ethics, History of," in *The New Catholic Encyclopedia*, Vol. 5 (New York, 1967), p. 574.

[17]Cahal B. Daly, *Natural Law Morality Today* (Dublin and London, 1965), 35.

Contrasting with situationism is an ethical system which holds for the existence of various unchanging moral principles, none of which may directly be violated if an individual's action is to be morally correct. Such an ethical approach generally goes under the name of natural law, although this may not be the most happy term for it, since the name lends itself to misinterpretation. It is all too easy, for example, to imagine that the "natural law" can be determined simply by a cursory inspection of human "nature"; having settled on the components of this "nature," one then proceeds mechanically to denominate actions as morally good or bad by measuring them for their consistency or inconsistency with "nature."

There are, however, more viable "natural law" theories available than this.[18] One illuminating approach turns to psychology and anthropology for evidence of the existence of a number of "basic human goods." These disciplines, it is said, although they differ in terminology and on just what to include and what to exclude from a list of such "goods," nevertheless reflect agreement on the existence of a number of fundamental human inclinations, such as the tendency to preserve life, the tendency to mate and raise children, the tendency to question and explore, and so on. The objects of these tendencies are the basic human goods. Practical reason, that is, reason concerned with what ought to be done, finds in these

[18]See, e.g., Germain G. Grisez, *Contraception and the Natural Law* (Milwaukee, 1964).

goods the starting points for working out the rules of behavior. An action which is always wrong is one which requires that the person performing it set his will against one or more of these basic goods. In doing so, an individual thereby also turns his will against one or more of the starting points of practical reason. Thus an immoral action of this kind is also fundamentally irrational. Taken all together, the basic human goods represent the sum total of possible human achievement. As fundamental principles and objects of human activity, they are absolutely indispensable for personal growth and the advancement of the human community.

Human life is one such good. One's will must always be oriented toward life and in its favor; turning against life directly is always and in itself evil. Thus, it would not be morally permissible to kill a sick man, even to end his suffering, for killing him would mean turning one's will directly against the basic human good of life. In this approach, of course, the goods may not be sacrificed to so-called "practical" considerations; an immoral course of action may in a given case seem to be the "realistic" one, while the moral course of action appears impractical. From a different point of view, however, it is the immoral action which is irrational because it involves turning against one of the starting points of practical reason. The point here is that evil lies in *turning against* one of the goods. Obviously, one cannot always be seeking all of the goods in each and every action one performs. But neither may one directly attack one or more of them, because all are equally basic (although not equally important: life, for instance, is certainly more important than many other goods). In a sense, an immoral action is one which puts too much emphasis on one good at the expense of others or another. Being equally basic, the goods may not be subordinated to one another. This is to make a false absolute of one of the goods at the expense of the others.

Direct abortion is an attack on human life. Inevitably, therefore, it involves a turning of the will against the good of human life. That is why direct abortion is always and everywhere wrong, according to a "natural law" theory of morality.

It should be stressed that such an approach to morality is not static. On the contrary, moral progress is only possible when it can be measured by fixed, unchanging standards.

Reflecting on some instances of actual progress will make this clear. Killing of the innocent is in all circumstances absolutely evil; but there can be both growing moral insight into the classification of "the innocent" and growing technical possibilities for preserving innocent life. The "closed" tribal moralities of primitive peoples tended to regard members of the tribe only as "innocent," and had little scruple in exterminating "enemies"; all but the tribal "in-group" being liable to be classified as enemies. There can be moral progress without limit in "opening" the concept of "innocent" until it includes, with ever fewer exceptions, "mankind of every description" and living human beings at every stage from conception to senility. Moral progress in this sense is never guaranteed, never unilinear, and is still, despite our heritage of civilization and Christianity, very rudimentary. There are more vestiges amongst us than we care to admit of tribal or "in-group" morality. But the point to notice is that progress, past or future, is never outside or beyond the absolute standard of respect for human life. Progress is openness *to* and never *beyond* the absolute standard.[19]

While it is true, as noted above, that individual Christian thinkers have at various times been prepared to accept abortion as morally permissible in some circumstances, it is equally true that the mainstream of Christian thought has throughout history rejected abortion as always wrong. This teaching extends from the time of the *Didache* to the present. Thus, in the Second Vatican Council's *Pastoral Constitution on the Church in the Modern World*, one reads:

For God, the Lord of life, has conferred on men the surpassing ministry of safeguarding life—a ministry which must be fulfilled in a manner which is worthy of man. Therefore from the moment of its conception life must be guarded with the greatest care, while abortion and infanticide are unspeakable crimes.[20]

[19]Daly, 10.
[20]*Pastoral Constitution on the Church in the Modern World*, #51, in Walter M. Abbott, S. J., ed., *The Documents of Vatican II* (New York, 1966; paperback edition), pp. 255-56.

THE QUESTION OF ANIMATION

An issue that has sometimes vexed moralists is that of animation—the question, that is, of when the fetus receives a human soul and so becomes fully human. In the nature of things, this seems destined to remain a permanently moot point; certainly no test presently available, or imaginable, to either medicine or theology is capable of settling the matter.

Nor should it be supposed that the issue is of practical importance for the morality of abortion. Directly intended termination of pregnancy is gravely wrong at any stage in the development of the fetus. But because the issue of animation is still sometimes raised, and because there is a danger that debate on this question may fog the central issue of the immorality of abortion, it is worthwhile examining the issue briefly to see what is really in dispute.

Aristotle taught that the fetus did not receive a spiritual soul at the moment of conception but only some time later. His theory was introduced into the Roman world by Galen, a Greek physician in the court of the Emperor Severus, and in one form or another came to be universally accepted. The most common opinion was that "animation," the infusion of the spiritual, properly human soul, did not occur until after forty days in the case of males and eighty days in the case of females. The terms "unformed" and "formed" are often used to describe the respective states of the fetus before and after animation.

Many theologians, including Augustine, Jerome and Aquinas, accepted this theory and distinguished between the animated and the nonanimated fetus. The same distinction was introduced into church law in the twelfth century by Gratian, who made it the basis for assessing penalties for abortion. Early in the seventeenth century, however, scientists began to speculate that the human soul was infused immediately after conception. Fairly soon this became a commonly accepted position among theologians. It remains so at the present day, although reputable defenders can be found for both points of view.

Thus, a contemporary argument for the "infusion" of the soul at a point subsequent to conception is based on "the necessary soul-body relationship":

> The human spirit is the principle of activity of an organic body that is properly disposed for truly human behavior. Such proximate dispositions would not be present if the body did not possess human organs for the organic faculties, the operations of which are indispensable for the exercise of reason. The time when such organ systems are present in the human fetus, especially the organization of the brain, must be ascertained by embryology and is probably not before the end of the third month after conception. It is likely that human animation takes place at this time.[21]

An equally contemporary argument for immediate "infusion" of the soul draws its support from the

[21]R. J. Nogar, "Evolution, Human. 2. Philosophical Aspects," in *The New Catholic Encyclopedia*, Vol. 5 (New York, 1967), p. 684.

"evidence of specifically human operations from the first moment of conception."

> . . . [M]odern studies in embryology reveal that at the moment sperm and ovum unite and the two pronuclei fuse, an orderly process of development begins with a definiteness governed by the pattern of the DNA molecule. The new individual is characterized by the resulting unique constellation of genes and chromosomes before the zygote divides for the first time. This organization is not only intricate and vital; it is specifically human. The chromosomes contain determiners for specifically human eyes and ears, not just animal eyes and ears in general. . . . Embryology considers the living body from the one-cell stage onward to be a human individual, not some general plant or animal that will become human in 40 or 80 days.[22]

What is at issue, of course, is the moment at which the fetus becomes a human person. As far as abortion is concerned, the question is relevant for establishing the exact nature of the moral wrong that is committed by one who seeks or performs abortion. If the fetus is fully human from the moment of conception, abortion at any stage is homicide. If, on the contrary, the fetus does not become human until some time after conception, abortion before that time will not be homicide; rather, its "predominant malice" would be "the frustration of the process of procreation, analogous to the malice of contraception."[23] "Malice"

[22]J. E. Royce, "Soul, Human, Origin of," in *The New Catholic Encyclopedia*, Vol. 13 (New York, 1967), p. 471.
[23]Francis J. Connell, C.SS.R., *More Answers To Today's Moral Problems* (Washington, D. C., 1965), p. 85.

here does not, of course, mean the same thing as "maliciousness" but refers instead to the particular category of wrongdoing which is involved. It is important, however, that even in the latter case the malice of abortion would only be "analogous" to that of contraception; there is a vast and morally significant difference between contraception and abortion, since contraception *prevents* conception while abortion destroys the *product* of conception, a far more serious matter because it is a more direct attack on human life.

In any case, the issue is not of practical significance so far as the morality of abortion is concerned. By any theory of "animation," abortion is gravely wrong. As one writer puts it, "every direct abortion is a sin of murder at least in intention, if not in actuality. It is probable, in fact almost certain, that every developing fetus is human. To kill what is probably human is murder."[24] A similar point is made by the Protestant moralist Paul Ramsey, Harrington Spear Professor of Religion at Princeton University. In a recent article[25] Ramsey suggests—without asserting—that the point at which individual human life begins could be that of the blastocyst; this is the stage early in fetal development at which the so-called "primitive streak" appears in the cluster of developing cells signaling separation into identical twins and prior to which,

[24]Anthony Zimmerman, S.V.D., *Catholic Viewpoint on Overpopulation* (Garden City, N. Y., 1961), pp. 137-38.

[25]Paul Ramsey, "The Sanctity of Life: In the First of It," *The Dublin Review*, Spring, 1967.

arguably, human individuation would not have occurred, at least in the case of such twins. But even
supposing that the stage of blastocyst is the point of
"animation," abortion prior to that time would be
wrong, Ramsey says. "Whenever the line is drawn, the
direct destruction of the foetus after that point will,
by definition, be murder, while before that point its
direct destruction would fall under some other
species of sin or grave violation." Having reviewed
"all these distinctions and theories about when germinating life becomes human," Ramsey adds, it is essential to note that "from an authentic religious point
of view none of them matters very much."

If one does not know with certainty that his action
is *not* killing a person, he is accepting responsibility
for doing so. One who is willing to kill what may or
may not be human is, by the very terms of the
proposition, willing to kill what *is* human. Hence one
who performs or consents to abortion inescapably
assumes the guilt of homicide. The point may be
somewhat more apparent if removed for the moment
from the context of homicide. Thus, one might say
that a man who drank a certain concoction without
knowing whether or not it was poisonous—but with
reason to believe that it *might* be poison—had a
suicidal attitude, since his action could only be interpreted as meaning that he was prepared to drink
what *was* poisonous. In the same manner, a man who
kills something which may or may not be human—
but which he has reason to believe *may* be human—

has a homicidal attitude, since his action demonstrates that he is prepared to kill what *is* human.

Furthermore, destruction of the fetus, whether or not it is yet a human person, is a "usurpation of God's sole right over the fruit of man's reproductive act. . . . Man may not interfere after positing the preconditions [for the creation of a soul], under pain of seriously offending the Creator."[26] As Ramsey says, "Every human being is a unique, unrepeatable opportunity to praise God. His life is entirely an ordination, a loan and a stewardship."[27] And again, quoting Karl Barth: "The unborn child is from the very first a child. . . . He who destroys germinating life kills a man and thus ventures the monstrous thing of decreeing concerning the life and death of a fellow-man whose life is given by God and therefore, like his own, belongs to Him."[28]

Even assuming, then, what cannot be proved— that the fetus does not receive a human soul until some time after conception—abortion remains gravely immoral. That this is the true content of Christian tradition is evident from the fact that even those theologians of the past who accepted theories of delayed animation still condemned abortion at any stage in the development of the fetus. "No scholastic drew the inference from the opinion of Aristotle that an abortion preceding the fortieth (or the eightieth)

[26]Zimmerman, *Viewpoint,* 137-38.
[27]Ramsey, "The Sanctity of Life."
[28]Quoted in Ramsey, "The Sanctity of Life."

day would not be a crime."[29] St. Alphonsus Liguori, although he believed in delayed animation, nevertheless held that abortion is *"per se* a mortal sin; and the person guilty of it is responsible for homicide."[30] The most relevant reaction is to restate two rather blunt comments, one dating from the fourth century, the other from the twentieth. The former is that of St. Basil, who stated that abortion is murder and no "hair-splitting distinction" about whether the fetus was "formed" or not could make it otherwise. The other is that of Dietrich Bonhoeffer, the Lutheran anti-Nazi theologian, who wrote:

> Destruction of the embryo in the mother's womb is a violation of the right to live which God has bestowed upon this nascent life. To raise the question whether we are here concerned already with a human being or not is merely to confuse the issue. The simple fact is that God certainly intended to create a human being and that this nascent human being has been deliberately deprived of his life. And that is nothing but murder.[31]

THE CHRISTIAN TRADITION

The condemnation of abortion looks simultaneously in two directions. It emphasizes the rights of both God and the unborn child. Abortion involves a "twofold violation of justice."[32] God's prerogatives enter

[29]Bernard Häring, C.SS.R., *The Law of Christ*, Vol. III—Special Moral Theology (Westminster, Md., 1966), p. 205.
[30]Quoted in Bouscaren, 42.
[31]Dietrich Bonhoeffer, *Ethics*, ed. Eberhard Bethge (New York, 1965; paperback edition), pp. 175-76.
[32]Zimmerman, *Viewpoint*, 136.

the picture because abortion is an infringement of His right to dispose as He will of the product of conception. Man is a creature, dependent on God for having come to be and for continuing in existence. His dominion over his own life and the lives of others is sharply limited. He has no right to take the life of another innocent human being. Such disposition of life belongs solely to God, its Creator. It is in this sense that abortion involves a violation of justice toward God.

In performing an abortion, a man sets himself up in the place of the Creator and presumes to dispose of life according to his own will. The modern age seems of course peculiarly ill-disposed to consider the rights of the Creator. Probably most advocates of abortion would not even regard this as a serious argument against the practice. Yet those at least who truly believe in God as Creator, and as Lord of what He has created, see that the direct destruction of innocent human life, whether by abortion or any other means, is gravely wrong. For them it is an operative principle that man is "not absolutely master of his own life and body. He has no *dominion* over it, but holds it in trust for God's purposes."[33] Says Father Bernard Häring, C.SS.R.:

> God alone is the Lord of life and death. No physician may pass and execute the sentence of death on one who is innocent. But he must do all that is in his

[33]Norman St. John-Stevas, *The Right to Life* (New York, 1964), p. 12.

power to save the life of the mother and child. If despite all his sincere efforts, based on the soundest training and most thorough experience, he is not successful, then God Himself has rendered the decision and passed the verdict on human life.[34]

Admittedly this has a harsh ring to contemporary ears. God passing a "verdict on human life"? How unspeakably medieval! On the other hand, what exactly is abortion if not a human verdict on human life? Abortion means nothing less than the substitution of human judgment for God's. This surely is the assumption of omnicompetence with a vengeance.

Of greater weight with those who support abortion is the argument based on the rights of the unborn child, or so it would appear from the amount of effort expended in trying to explain away these rights or show that somehow they do not really exist after all. The notion of an invasion of God's rights is perhaps difficult to grasp or to picture, but it is not at all difficult to understand what it means to violate the rights of another human being, particularly when the right involved is so fundamental and so obvious as the right to life. For this reason most defenses of abortion, if they aspire to logic, become involved in the effort to show that the unborn child has no rights, or at least that his rights are somehow inferior to those of his parents and may therefore be violated when this seems either necessary or expedient to advance the parents' interests.

[34]Häring, 209.

The most obvious attempt along these lines is the denial that the unborn child is a separate entity with rights of his own. It is argued—or, more truly perhaps, asserted—that before birth the child is simply a part of the mother's body, as if he were only another organ or member. And since everyone agrees that an individual organ may be removed if this is required for the welfare of the body as a whole, it follows, according to this line of thought, that abortion, the removal of the unborn, non-viable child, is permitted when this is required for the mother's physical or mental well-being (or merely perhaps for her convenience). The analogy involved here is of course false and misleading on its face. If the fetus is merely a "part" of the mother's body, it is certainly a very unusual, indeed remarkable, part. No other "part" of the body becomes a human being in its own right, as the fetus does. The Christian tradition, however, has always rejected the notion that the fetus is part of the mother's body. As one moralist has written:

> . . . [There] is direct and unbroken continuity of life from the fertilization of the ovum to the development of the embryo, foetus, infant, child, youth, and man. Any distinct and living organism, fundamentally capable of intelligence, is a human person and remains such as long as it possesses life.[35]

The same position is taken by medical science, except, of course, by those members of the profession

[35]Thomas J. Higgins, S. J., *Man as Man*, revised ed. (Milwaukee, 1958), 251.

who have become advocates for abortion. Thus one medical writer says:

> Biologically as well as ethically the only logical and satisfactory view of the embryo is to regard it as a human being from the outset. It has from the outset a degree of independence with regard to the mode of its growth and development and, though receiving nutrition from the mother, the manner of its development is not controlled by her. . . . It is from the outset a human being.[36]

It is also from the outset something genetically unique, a being obviously quite distinct from the mother. The genetic makeup of its cells takes elements from the mother and elements from the father and combines these into an altogether new, unique pattern which is characteristically its own and which distinguishes it from either parent.

It is, as a matter of fact, hard to see why the question of whether or not the fetus is independent of the mother should be regarded as at all determinative. For months and years *after* birth, children are incapable of surviving "independently," if this means providing the necessities of life for themselves. The same is true of severely sick people and many elderly persons. By the logic of an argument based on "independence," newborn children, invalids and the aged should also be subject to destruction upon the demonstration of need or convenience. The unborn

[36]John Marshall, M.D., *Medicine and Morals* (Glen Rock, N. J., 1964), p. 66.

child, of course, lives within the womb, the others outside it; but the accident of environment seems a rather flimsy ground on which to base a decision for the destruction of innocent life. One might with equal logic argue that elderly persons who can afford to live in their own homes may be spared, but those obliged to seek public housing or live with children or other relatives should be destroyed. Birth, the severing of the umbilical cord and other suggested dividing lines are merely arbitrary points in the development of the child.[37] They are irrelevant so far as his being an entity separate and distinct from his mother is concerned.

One may agree with Pastor Richard John Neuhaus that it is "profoundly disturbing" to hear proponents of abortion dismiss such considerations "in a cavalier manner."

> Pre-natal life is denigrated as a "piece of tissue," "a woman's mistake," or "vegetating unborn matter." Such language begs the question in a disgraceful manner. Biology and everyday experience teach us that life is to be understood in continuity with life. As one biologist states it, "birth is but a convenient landmark in a continuous process". . . . The casual claim that "of course" and "obviously" there is a difference between the fetus and the baby is supported only by the wish for a simple resolution of a troubling problem.[38]

As Paul Ramsey remarks, the pro-abortionists' ef-

[37]*Ibid.*
[38]Richard John Neuhaus, "The Dangerous Assumptions," *Commonweal*, June 30, 1967.

forts to establish criteria for human life are hopelessly wide of the mark, since they would exclude altogether too much.

> The human infant acquires its personhood and self-conscious subjective identity through "Thou-I" encounters with other selves; and a child acquires essential rationality even more laboriously. If life must be human in these senses before it has any sanctity and respect or rights due it, this would seem to justify infanticide under any number of conditions believed to warrant this as permissible behavior or as a social policy.[39]

The mentality which seeks to deny status as a human being to the child until he has reached some purely arbitrary point of development is a strange one which resembles in some ways that of the primitive tribes which respect only the lives of fellow tribesmen but have no compunction about killing one who has not been initiated into the tribe. This "in-group" mentality seeks to deny basic rights to outsiders and bases the denial on the argument that the outsiders are somehow not fully human or have not reached the same level of humanity as the members of the privileged caste. This was the argument employed by the Nazis against the Jews; it is the argument used today by racists of every variety. And it is the argument of those who endorse abortion, because the unborn child is somehow not human—or not as human as the rest of us.

[39]Ramsey, "The Sanctity of Life."

The radical weakness of the argument appears when it is pushed to its logical conclusions. Thus, assuming that birth is the magic point at which the child suddenly becomes human, is one to suppose that a child who is only one-third of the way out of the womb may be killed, but one who is two-thirds of the way out may not? Is the child's life sacred five minutes after labor begins but subject to destruction five minutes before? The fact that the argument permits the asking of such questions illustrates how ludicrous it is. By contrast, the humane, civilized tradition has always been to regard the child's life as protected from the moment of conception by the same guarantees that surround every human life. Personality and the rights that go with it are not conferred by men. They are inalienable rights, which no other human being or human society has power to give to or withdraw from the child.

More frequently invoked perhaps than the attempt to show that the unborn child is not a separate entity, and hence has no rights, is the argument that his right to life must give way to the mother's rights— whether to life, good health, comfort or convenience is not always specified—in cases of apparent conflict. This raises the very fundamental issue of how one regards human life. Are all lives equal, or are some lives, in George Orwell's famous phrase, "more equal than others"? Apparently the proponents of abortion regard the mother's right to life as "more equal" than the child's. They feel, in other words, that it takes precedence over the child's right.

But it is paradoxical, to say the least, that such a doctrine of inequality should find support at a time when the essential equality of all human beings regardless of accidental factors is being recognized and preached with fervor the world over. The unborn, it would seem, is the only minority left against whom it is possible to discriminate with impunity. Others claim and defend their rights vociferously; only those unborn are voiceless.

The Christian tradition rejects the notion that one life can take precedence over another. Human beings *are* equal. There are no exceptions. Recognition of this fact caused Pope Pius XII to declare that innocent human life is "withdrawn from the very first moment of its existence from any direct deliberate attack."[40]

To the argument that the life of the mother is of "incomparably greater value" than that of the child, Pius responded flatly that "the inviolability of the life of an innocent human being does not depend upon its greater or lesser value." The attempt to assign values to human lives and then act accordingly opens the door to every sort of violation and injustice. As one moralist has written:

> The general thrust of the repeated teaching of Catholic (and Judeo-Christian) tradition is this: one cannot put a price on human life. As soon as one

[40]Address to the Family Front, November 26, 1951.

allows direct suppression of innocent human life in any form, he has priced human life. That is, he has subordinated it to some temporal value: economic advantage, physical well being, the good life, protection of reputation or whatever it may be. Once he has done this, there is nothing *in principle* that prevents his destroying human life at other stages and in other circumstances: the aged, the infirm, the socially or economically burdensome, the crippled, the suffering. It is only a matter of waiting until the going price has been reached.[41]

Pricing human life: that is what abortion means. Who feels himself competent to set that price? The question is neither academic nor rhetorical—as witness the recent controversy in Great Britain over the disclosure that a London hospital had set broad categories of patients who were not to be resuscitated if their hearts stopped beating.[42] Admittedly, there are extreme cases where the prolongation of life is not morally required and may, in fact, be pointless and cruel. In the case of the Neasden Hospital, however, it appears that a blanket edict existed against the resuscitation of patients who were over sixty-five, "very elderly," or who suffered from malignancies, chronic chest disease or chronic kidney disease. Such a policy can only be interpreted as reflecting the attitude that certain people's lives are not worth living and should be allowed to terminate at the earliest possible opportunity. And this in turn suggests just

[41]Richard A. McCormick, S. J., "Abortion," *America*, June 19, 1965.
[42]*The New York Times*, September 23 and 24, 1967.

how far our society already may be along the way toward an ambivalent attitude toward the right to life. It does not seem in the least alarmist to suggest that the next step beyond abortion—euthanasia—is a good deal nearer at hand than many people suspect.

MOTHER OR CHILD?

One of the charges thrown in the faces of those who oppose abortion is that as a matter of fact *they* prefer the life of the unborn child to that of the mother. They are said to do this because they refuse to sanction abortion even in those cases of difficult births—now, fortunately, more often spoken of than actually seen in modern medical practice—in which the delivery of a living child will mean the death of the mother. It is not true, however, that opposition to abortion in such cases means giving the child's life preference over the mother's. As Pius XII stated, "Never and in no case has the Church taught that the life of the child must be preferred to the life of the mother."[43] In such cases, the Pope said, there is "but one obligation: to make every effort to save the lives of both, of the mother and of the child." And if the case is actually hopeless, he added, "nothing else remains for the man, who will make every effort till the very last moment to help and save, but to bow respectfully before the laws of nature and the dispositions of Divine Providence." Elaborating on this teaching, a recent writer has commented:

[43]Address to the Family Front, November 26, 1951.

The morality of an act cannot be judged by its practical results. Ethics cannot be based upon the premise that to save one life is better than none, two lives better than one and so on, without any regard for means by which the lives are preserved. In the present case two lives may be lost. It is possible to save one of these lives. To do this the other life must be directly destroyed, a life which is innocent and helpless to defend itself. Can this be considered right or just, or preferable to doing everything possible to save both lives, even though one may be defeated in the end? One cannot cut one's losses with regard to human life as on the stock market or in business.[44]

"The life of each is equally sacred," declared Pius XI.[45] Neither may be preferred, neither directly destroyed.

This position does, however, leave room for so-called indirect abortion, in which the death of the unborn child is neither directly intended nor directly sought, but merely results as a side effect of some other morally allowable action. An example is surgery to remove the cancerous womb of a pregnant woman. In such a case, a non-viable fetus will surely die. But its death is neither intended nor sought. A general test is whether or not the same operation might be performed on a non-pregnant woman in the same therapeutic circumstances. The treatment does not aim at termination of pregnancy as its objective, but rather at some therapeutic goal unrelated to the fact that the patient is pregnant. There must,

[44]Marshall, *Medicine and Morals*, pp. 77-78.
[45]*Casti Connubii.*

of course, be a grave reason for the course of action
that results in the death of the fetus, a reason comparable in gravity to this unintended, unsought sacrifice
of innocent life. Those who hold this position judge
that it is no departure from their absolute opposition
to abortion, since what they are in fact opposing is
the *direct* taking of innocent life. "Were it proved to
their satisfaction that the excisions in question constitute direct killing in the moral sense, they would
disallow them and stand by the principle."[46]

As a practical matter, abortion involves an added
aspect of evil in that it is usually brought about by
people who have an added obligation in the opposite
direction. By the nature of their vocation, parents and
physicians assume a special duty to protect and preserve human life. By cooperating in an abortion they
set themselves against the very value for which they
should be concerned. Similarly, one is shocked at en-
countering a perversion of justice in any circumstances; but there is a special aura of moral corrup-
tion in the case of a judge who is disclosed to
have taken a bribe in return for rendering a favorable
verdict. This sense of special outrage arises from the
realization that the individual in question has been
guilty not merely of a generalized dishonesty but of
a special dereliction of duty arising from his special
obligation to cherish and protect the sanctity of the

[46]L. L. McReavy, "Abortion" (review of *Abortion, An
Ethical Discussion*), *Catholic Marriage Advisory Council
Bulletin,* Vol. 6, No. 1 (1966).

law. So from this point of view, the special obligation of the parties involved, abortion is in fact "something worse than murder."[47] The ordinary murderer has after all taken on no special obligations toward human life beyond those he shares with every other human being. But a parent or a doctor has, and that makes abortion especially wrong for him.

Abortion is a turning of the will against life, one of the most fundamental of the "basic human goods." These goods are simultaneously objects of inclination and values perceived as such by the practical reason; they should provide the moral orientation for all of human life. In turning against one of them, one turns against something which gives meaning to life. This is at the very heart of irrationality and immorality.

In a sense, abortion is not just *a* crime; rather, it, or the attitude of which it is a symptom, may be *the* characteristic crime of the twentieth century. Our times have lost respect for human life. Dachau, Hiroshima—these are landmarks testifying to how cheaply life is held today. And now one finds the same attitude of disrespect for human life, whether in the hospital that sets predetermined categories of patients who automatically will not be resuscitated, or in the arguments of those who find in an abortion a quick and easy solution to difficulties. The supporters of abortion do not, of course, announce themselves, or even think of themselves, as enemies of human life. Honorable men, they bolster their cause with hu-

[47]Zimmerman, *Viewpoint,* 136.

mane slogans: "Protect the mother's health"; "Save
the child from the stigma of illegitimacy." Naturally,
no one quarrels with such objectives. But does a good
end make any and every means to it legitimate?
Means have their own moral quality, and if they are
immoral they may not be chosen. No one is in favor
of the suffering that results from poverty, illegitimacy, or other social and personal misfortunes. But
it is immoral and inhuman to try to eradicate suffering by methods which themselves involve trampling
on essential human values and rights.

> . . . [T]he avoidance of pain is not a very strong
> case when balanced . . . against the seriousness of
> taking human life. Respect for human rights is fre-
> quently inconvenient. As harsh as it may sound to
> some, the just and prudent law is not always the
> easy law.[48]

It may very well be, as Paul Ramsey says, that the
controversy over abortion and the law will become
irrelevant once the abortion pills now being developed become generally available. Abortion then
will be an issue in a private sphere which law cannot
reach.

> Already the fashionable women's magazines speak
> of this; and the name for the procedure is the "M-pill"
> not the "A-pill." This is to say that euphemistically
> any woman will be able to keep herself systematically
> ignorant of whether she is with some frequency per-
> forming an abortion on herself. She need not face
> the question of whether she should do *that*. She only

[48]Neuhaus, "The Dangerous Assumptions."

need imagine, she will be systematically tempted to believe, that she is only doing what comes naturally every month.[49]

Indeed, this state of affairs may already be at hand if the intrauterine devices and birth control drugs now on the market actually produce their effect by preventing the implantation of the fertilized ovum in the uterus, in which case they are acting as abortifacients. Those who oppose abortion face the serious obligation of stressing, in season and out, that abortion is not simply another medical procedure, such as tonsillectomy, to be discussed on its merits as a therapeutic technique, nor an instrument of socioeconomic betterment, like a raise or cut in taxes, subject to political bartering, but is instead a radical attack both on the principle of the sanctity of human life and on individual, already existing human lives.

Abortion, as this study has shown, is in many cases not even an effective means to such good ends as mental and physical health. But even if it were a universally effective panacea, it would still be wrong, and no slogans could make it otherwise. Reasonable men look beyond slogans to the reality of what is being proposed. If the suggested "price" is innocent

[49]Paul Ramsey, "Some Terms of Reference for the Abortion Debate," paper delivered at an International Conference on Abortion, sponsored by the Harvard Divinity School in Cooperation with the Joseph P. Kennedy, Jr., Foundation, September 6-8, 1967, in Washington, D.C.

human life, it cannot be paid. Every human life is infinitely precious. Abortion cheapens life. Our times have seen human life devalued too often already. It must not happen again in the name of abortion.

VII

The Abortion Controversy

It is not the purpose of this book to outline a comprehensive strategy and tactics by which those who oppose abortion should meet the current challenge to their position. The objective, rather, has been to examine the issues commonly raised in debate on abortion and point out the merit (or lack of merit) in frequently heard arguments. This treatment would, however, be incomplete without at least some reference to tactical issues, particularly since the opponents of abortion seem to have a certain talent for getting tangled in these and often end up wasting their energies in intramural quarrels.

In particular, several non-issues seem to crop up with great frequency in discussions and generate much more heat than light. Among them are the following:

1. *Opposition to abortion stirs up interreligious friction and is a blow to hard-won ecumenical gains.* The conclusion, though it is not always stated, is that public opposition to abortion, or at least to changes in the laws on abortion, should therefore be abandoned.

The fundamental assumption here is that the controversy over abortion is one of Roman Catholics versus the house. In a strict sense, however, this is not true. A number of non-Roman Catholic religious figures—several of them cited in the preceding pages —are also opposed to abortion and to changes in the abortion laws. Opposition to abortion is therefore de facto simply not a "Roman Catholic" position.

Realistically, however, it is true that the largest single bloc of opposition to changing the abortion laws is composed of Catholics. Does it therefore follow that Catholics who are active in this area are un-ecumenical or that they should abandon their efforts for the sake of interfaith harmony?

The question of the ecumenical commitment of Catholic opponents of abortion is one to which, in the nature of things, no sensible answer can be given. Ecumenical credentials are not that accessible to inspection. One might, however, hazard the guess that, if they were, those of the Catholics who are active in their opposition to abortion would show that their generally high level of religious and civic involvement makes them rather more ecumenically oriented than the average Christian.

A much more substantial question is whether opposition to abortion should be dropped where it provokes friction among religious groups. Here the comment of the Jesuit editors of *America* on "tough" ecumenism is pertinent: "If ecumenism is to mean letting everyone have his way, we will have fallen into the trap of substituting a ridiculous laissez faire for the true goal of religious unity."[1] Certainly one of the essentials of ecumenism is learning not only how to agree but, at least initially, how to disagree, while at the same time respecting those with whom one disagrees and working to narrow the area of disagreement. Ecumenism which papers over fundamental differences is risking eventual disaster, for differences are not removed in this way but are only temporarily hidden.

It remains perfectly true, however, that ecumenism, and good manners and respect for the democratic process, demand that disagreements be expressed fairly and charitably. On the abortion question: there is nothing wrong with those who regard abortion as the destruction of innocent human life calling abortion "murder," because in this view of it, that is exactly what it is; there is, however, a great deal wrong with calling those who argue for the acceptability of abortion, "murderers." A murderer, after all, knows and feels that he is committing murder. This is scarcely the case with those who favor abortion. Thus the word "murderer" might profitably be dropped from the debate over abortion, as might references to the "insensitivity," "medieval mentality" and so forth of those who oppose abortion. The air would be a good deal clearer if it could be generally accepted that the issue is one on which well-meaning men can disagree.

[1]"Abortion Debate and 'Tough' Ecumenism," *America*, March 11, 1967.

2. Related to the ecumenical non-issue is the argument that *opponents of abortion should not try to impose their views on others through legislation.* People who favor changes in the abortion laws, it is said, do not contemplate making abortion compulsory for anyone. Why, then, should those who oppose changes try to make non-abortion compulsory?

To understand the attitude on this point of those who oppose abortion, it is necessary to understand how they view the act of abortion itself. In their view, abortion is not simply a private matter involving a woman, a man, a doctor and nobody else. There is another interest: that of the unborn child. And the protection of the child's right to life is very properly an object of the concern of the law. From this perspective, the "imposing" is on the side of those who favor abortion, since they are imposing death on an innocent human life.

As a further refinement on this non-issue, it is sometimes suggested that something in the American constitutional tradition makes it inappropriate for those who have religious objections to abortion to seek to have their viewpoint embodied in law. No other group of Americans, however, is expected to drop their deepest commitments when they enter the area of public policy, and it is a bit difficult to see why those with religious commitments should be obliged to do so. More to the point, perhaps, the issue of abortion law inevitably involves one's most fundamental views on human life and human destiny. These views may or may not correspond with those of a particular religion, but they are, willy-nilly, in a true sense "religious." In this sense, those who favor abortion may be said to do so on "religious" grounds, because of their view of how and when human life begins, or of what disposition may be made of human life once it has begun, or of what sort of human life is worth living. There is no such thing as a non-religious view on abortion, and no law on abortion, whether for or against, is devoid of religious content.

Passing beyond the non-issues, it is worth commenting here on one suggested response to the current pressure for change in the law. This is that those who oppose abortion nevertheless be prepared to accept—and even to propose—modifications to permit abortion in such cases as rape or suspected fetal abnormality. It is suggested that this sort of minimal concession to the presumptively inevitable would delay and perhaps forestall entirely efforts to obtain the enactment of even more permissive legislation.

One can readily grant that, if this tactic would in fact prevent the passage of more permissive laws, it should be adopted. When in politics one has the option of choosing the lesser of two evils, and choice is unavoidable, one should certainly do so. The question is, however, whether the tactic would in fact prevent what it seeks to prevent, namely, the eventual enactment of laws permitting abortion in an even broader range of circumstances.

No one has the answer to this question. It is, however, beyond doubt that, as was pointed out in the first chapter of this book, the most ardent proponents of abortion will rest content with nothing less than abortion on demand. They view the currently proposed modifications of the law merely as preliminary steps along the way to this goal, designed to condition legislatures and public opinion to the abortion idea. Perhaps their strategy will not work. It is certain, however, that they intend to press it hard. It is also well within the realm of possibility that acceptance of some modifications in the law to make it easier to obtain an abortion would, rather than forestalling their efforts, simply make their work easier for them.

What, finally, should be the response of opponents of abortion in states which enact liberalized laws? Again, the answer is suggested by those who favor abortion on demand. Part of their strategy is to press for liberal interpretation of "moderate" laws, by the medical and legal professions, by the courts, and by the public, so that, even in advance of additional legislative action, abortion on demand will become a de facto reality. In these circumstances, the obvious response is to press for as restrictive an interpretation as possible. If the law says abortion is permitted to save a woman's life, then abortions should be tolerated only in cases where they are demonstrably needed to save lives. If the law says abortion is permitted where a child is likely to be born with grave deformity, then abortions should be tolerated only in cases where there is real medical evidence that such deformities are likely. Insistence on this sort of strict observance of the law is in the first instance the responsibility of doctors; beyond that line of defense, it is the duty of lawyers and judges.

The abortion controversy is, in any realistic view of things, likely to be prolonged and unpleasant. There will be ample opportunity for those who oppose abortion to become discouraged or simply to grow weary of the whole disagreeable subject. The stakes, however, are terribly high—as high as human life itself. There are very few better reasons for persevering in a fight than that.

Index